THE ADVICE-BASED BANKER™

GUIDING CREDIT UNION MEMBERS FOR LIFE

Chad W. Maze

First edition

Published by **Discipline of Banking Press**
United States of America

ISBN: 979-8-9956359-0-1 (paperback)
ISBN: 979-8-9956359-1-8 (eBook)
ISBN: 979-8-9956359-2-5 (audiobook)
Library of Congress Control Number: 2026909189

Printed in the United States of America

Discipline of Banking Press is an imprint of Camino De Oro Enterprises, LLC.

DEDICATION

For Jackson

As you begin your career in banking, you will quickly discover that this work can be both challenging and deeply rewarding. You will learn more than you expect, meet people from every walk of life, and be invited into moments that matter more than numbers or paperwork ever could. You will sit across from people who are trying to make sense of important decisions, often without realizing how much courage it took for them to ask for help.

If you choose to remain in banking, your perspective will change. What begins as a job will gradually become a profession. You will stop seeing yourself as someone who processes transactions and start seeing yourself as someone who guides decisions. Someone people trust. Someone they return to when the stakes feel real.

And if you choose this path for the long term, I hope you come to see something even deeper. Banking, at its best, is the care of something entrusted to you. The judgment you develop, the lessons you learn, and the wisdom you earn are not meant to be kept to yourself. They are meant to be shared, with members who need clarity, with colleagues who are learning, and someday with those who will follow in your footsteps.

As your father, I am proud of the person you are becoming .
As your boss, I believe deeply in the banker you can be.

I hope this career challenges you, grounds you, and gives you a chance to make a meaningful difference, one conversation at a time. Enjoy the journey, and never lose sight of why it matters.

Pops

PROLOGUE

The Conversation That Changed Everything

Early in my career, I watched a young couple sit down with a banker in a credit union branch.

They were dressed like they had come from work. The husband had a folder tucked under his arm, the kind people bring when they want to seem prepared, even when they aren't sure what they're preparing for.

They looked excited. But also a little nervous.

The husband leaned forward and said:

> "We think we're ready to buy our first home."

The banker smiled and nodded. Then she did what she was trained to do.

She began explaining mortgage products.

Fixed rates.
Adjustable rates.
Loan terms.
Down payment requirements.

She knew her material. She spoke clearly and confidently. She was, by every visible measure, doing her job well.

The couple listened politely.

They nodded along.

They asked a few small questions.

But something felt off. The conversation had the shape of a presentation. The couple wasn't leaning in anymore. They were leaning back, politely absorbing information they hadn't quite asked for yet.

Then, after a few minutes, the wife spoke up.

She waited for a pause, and then said quietly:

> "We're not actually sure we can afford a house yet."

The room went still for a moment.

Then she added something I've never forgotten.

> "We were hoping someone could help us figure that out."

The banker recovered gracefully. She shifted gears, pulled up some numbers, and the conversation eventually found its footing. The couple left with information they could use.

But something had been lost in those first few minutes.

Not because the banker did anything wrong. She was knowledgeable. Professional. Helpful in the traditional sense.

What she missed wasn't a product. It wasn't a policy. It was a question.

One simple question, asked before the presentation began, might have changed everything.

> What brings you in today?
>
> Or even just: What are you trying to figure out?

Because the couple wasn't there for a mortgage.

They were there because they were standing at the edge of the biggest financial decision of their lives, and they didn't know if they were ready.

They wanted someone to help them think it through. Someone to ask them the right questions. Someone to look at their situation honestly and say: here's what I see, here's what to consider, here's what a next step might look like.

They wanted guidance before they wanted a product.

And that distinction, small as it might seem, is what this entire book is about.

I've thought about that couple many times over the years. Not because they were poorly served, they weren't, not really. But because that moment showed me something that I've watched play out thousands of times since in branches, in training rooms, in conversations with bankers at every level of experience.

Most people don't walk into a credit union because they want a financial product.

They walk in because they are trying to make a decision. Sometimes it's a small one. Sometimes it's one of the most significant decisions of their life. But in almost every case, what they're really hoping for, even if they can't quite say it, is someone who can help them think clearly about what comes next.

Someone who will ask before they answer.

Someone who will listen before they recommend.

Someone they can trust.

That person is sitting across the desk from them.

And when a banker understands that, really understands it, not just as a philosophy but as a way of showing up every day, something changes.

The conversations get better.

The relationships begin to form.

And eventually, members start saying something every banker quietly hopes to hear.

> "I wanted to talk to you before I made this decision."

That sentence is the goal.

Not the biggest loan closed. Not the most accounts opened. That sentence, from a member who trusts you enough to bring you their uncertainty before they act on it.

Because in that moment, you are no longer just the person who works at the credit union.

You have become their banker.

A NOTE FROM THE AUTHOR

I have spent thirty years working inside banks and credit unions, as an executive, a leader, and someone who has sat in enough branch conversations to know specifically what separates a banker members remember from one they forget.

Those thirty years have taken me through roles from teller to Chief Operating Officer at both community banks and credit unions. I've hired bankers and developed them. I've watched talented people plateau because nobody ever told them what the best bankers actually do differently. And I've watched others, some with no particular advantage in experience or credentials, build careers that members talk about for years, simply because they understood something fundamental about the work.

They understood that the conversation comes before the product.

That insight isn't complicated. But it isn't automatic either. It has to be practiced, and it has to be taught, and in my experience, it rarely is. Most training programs focus on products, processes, and compliance. They cover what bankers need to know. Very few address how great bankers actually show up in a room, or why some members will wait for a specific person while others treat every desk as interchangeable.

That gap is why I wrote this book.

Helping bankers become great is not something I do alongside my work. It is my work. It is, I believe, a calling, one that has shaped everything I've done in this industry. The ideas in these pages come from what I've observed, what I've taught, and what I've seen make a real difference in the lives of members and the careers of the bankers who serve them.

This book is for the banker who wants to be more than competent. Who wants to be the one members come back to. Who wants, someday, to hear a member say:

"I wanted to talk to you before I made this decision."

That's the banker this book is about. And with the right approach, it's the banker you will see in yourself.

Chad Maze

TABLE OF CONTENTS

The Advice-Based Banker ™

THE ADVICE-BASED BANKER™

INTRODUCTION

THE BANKER MEMBERS ACTUALLY WANT

On a Tuesday morning, a member walks into a credit union branch.

He's in his early forties, wearing a work jacket with a company logo on the chest. He looks like someone who knows what he wants and doesn't have a lot of time. He approaches a banker's desk, sits down, and gets right to it.

"I think I might need an auto loan."

This moment happens thousands of times every day in credit unions across the country. A member arrives with a request. A banker receives it.

What happens next is where everything diverges.

BANKER ONE

The banker smiles and reaches for her keyboard.

She's efficient. She's been through this hundreds of times. She asks the questions she's trained to ask.

What vehicle are you looking at?

What's the purchase price?

How much are you putting down?

What term were you thinking?

He answers each one. She types. Within a few minutes the application is underway, the numbers are in the system, and the approval comes back clean.

She walks him through the terms. He signs where indicated. She hands him a copy of the paperwork and thanks him for his membership.

He leaves with an auto loan.

The whole thing took maybe twelve minutes.

And by any reasonable measure, the banker did her job. She was professional. She was accurate. She got him what he asked for without wasting his time.

But here's what she never found out.

She never found out that his current truck, the one he's been driving for nine years, finally gave out last week. That he'd been limping it along for months, spending more on repairs than he wanted to admit. That he has a long commute and two kids he drops off at school, and reliability isn't a preference, it's a necessity.

She never found out that he wasn't sure what he could actually afford. That he'd done some rough math in his head but hadn't sat down with anyone to work through the real numbers. That he was a little anxious about taking on a payment and was half-hoping someone would help him think it through.

She never asked. He never offered. The transaction closed.

But the conversation never really started.

BANKER TWO

Now imagine the same man, same Tuesday morning, sitting down with a different banker.

He says the same thing.

"I think I might need an auto loan."

The banker smiles. But instead of reaching for her keyboard, she leans forward slightly and asks:

"What kind of vehicle are you thinking about?"

Something shifts. He sits up a little. Starts talking about a truck he's been looking at, a specific model, the one with the towing capacity he needs for a trailer he bought last summer. He's been researching it for a while.

She nods. Then asks:

"What made now the right time to start looking?"

And now he tells her about the repairs. The reliability issue. The school drop-offs. She listens without rushing him.

After a few minutes, she says something he wasn't expecting.

> *"Before we look at loan options, would it be helpful to figure out what monthly payment would actually feel comfortable for you? Sometimes that shapes the decision about which vehicle makes the most sense."*

He agrees, a little relieved.

They spend a few minutes looking at the numbers together, his income, his current expenses, what's already coming out each month. She shows him two or three scenarios at different price points. Explains the trade-offs simply, without jargon.

He ends up choosing a loan that's slightly more modest than he originally had in mind. Not because he couldn't qualify for more. Because once he saw the numbers clearly, the more conservative option felt right. It fit. It didn't stretch.

He thanks her before he leaves. And he means it, not the polite, transactional thanks of someone who got paperwork processed, but the thanks of someone who feels like they made a good decision.

TWO VERY DIFFERENT OUTCOMES

Here's the thing: both bankers approved an auto loan. Both were professional. Both completed the transaction correctly.

But only one of them helped him.

And that difference, invisible on a spreadsheet, impossible to capture in a monthly report, is what this book is about.

Because something happens after an experience like the second one. It's not immediate. It doesn't show up that day, or even that month. But when the member faces the next financial decision, a refinance, a home improvement loan, a question about a savings account, he doesn't just go back to the credit union.

He goes back to her.

I should probably talk to her before I do anything.

That thought is the goal. Not the loan. The thought.

Because when a member trusts you enough to bring you their uncertainty before they act, the relationship has fundamentally changed. You are no longer a service provider completing a transaction. You have become part of how they think about their financial life.

THE PRESSURE IN THE ROOM

Before we go further, I want to name something honestly.

If you work in a branch, you already know that conversations like the one Banker Two had aren't always easy to have. There are days when the lobby is full and the line is long and your manager is watching the board. There are members who come in wanting to get in and out in five minutes and don't particularly want to be asked how they're doing financially. There are moments when slowing down to ask a thoughtful question feels like a luxury the pace of the day won't allow.

That's real. This book won't pretend otherwise.

But here's what's also true: the bankers who take the time, even a few extra minutes, even a few more questions, are the ones who build the practices that make this job genuinely rewarding. They're the ones members come back to. They're the ones who get asked for by name. They're the ones who, a few years into their career, find that opportunities seem to follow them, because they've spent that time turning transactions into relationships, one conversation at a time.

Advice-based banking isn't a slower way to do the same job. It's a different understanding of what the job actually is.

WHAT THE JOB ACTUALLY IS

Most people don't walk into a credit union because they want a financial product.

They walk in because they are trying to accomplish something. Buy something. Solve something. Prepare for something. And underneath the specific request, the auto loan, the credit card, the question about a savings rate, there is almost always a larger situation they're navigating. A life event. A worry. A goal they haven't quite figured out how to reach.

The request is the surface. ***The conversation is the job.***

Credit unions understand this better than most financial institutions, because they were built around a different idea. Not customers. Members. That word isn't just branding, it reflects a founding conviction that the people who walk through the door deserve someone who is genuinely looking out for them. Someone who will help them make a good financial decision, not just a fast one.

That's the role. And it's worth taking seriously.

Because retail bankers aren't just the front line of the institution. They are, in a very real sense, the first stewards of judgment in the system. Before the underwriting model, before the credit policy, before the approval or denial, there is a conversation. The quality of that conversation shapes what gets decided, how the member feels about it, and whether they'll ever come back.

That's not a small thing. That's the whole thing.

THE BANKER THIS BOOK IS ABOUT

Every branch has one or two bankers who seem to do this naturally. Members gravitate toward them. People wait for them, even when another banker is available. They get asked for by name.

It's tempting to assume these bankers are just more outgoing, or more experienced, or simply better with people. Sometimes that's part of it. But if you watch closely, what you actually see is something more specific, and more learnable.

They ask questions before they offer answers. They listen in a way that makes people feel like their situation is being taken seriously. They explain things simply, without making members feel talked down to. And they seem genuinely interested, not in closing a transaction, but in the person sitting across from them.

That's the discipline this book is built around.

It's called member guidance. And the core of it is simple enough to say in three words:

Advice before products.

Understand the person before recommending the solution. Help them think clearly before offering the tool. When you do that consistently, something changes in how members experience you, and in how you experience the work.

WHAT THIS BOOK WILL SHOW YOU

This book is a practical guide to becoming the banker members trust.

It will show you the mindset that separates advisors from order-takers. The Banker Truths that shape how exceptional bankers think about their role. A simple framework, the Advice-Based Banker Pyramid, that explains how trust is built one conversation at a time. The five conversations that appear in every branch, every day, and how to guide each one. The questions that open doors. And what it looks like, concretely, to build a reputation for advice over the course of a career.

None of it requires a different personality. None of it requires aggressive selling, in fact, it requires the opposite.

It requires curiosity. A genuine interest in the person across the desk and what they're actually trying to figure out.

That's the place every great conversation starts.

THE BANKER MEMBERS REMEMBER

Years from now, the members you help will not remember the interest rate on their loan. They won't remember the fee structure or the exact terms of the agreement.

But they will remember how it felt to sit across from you.

Whether they felt rushed or heard. Whether they left more confused than when they arrived, or whether something that had felt complicated suddenly felt clear. Whether they walked out having been sold something, or having made a decision they understood and felt good about.

That experience, the felt quality of the conversation, is what determines whether someone comes back. Whether they bring their spouse. Whether they recommend you to a friend.

The banker this book is about is the one members remember.

And with the right approach, that banker is who you can become.

PART I

THE MINDSET OF AN ADVICE-BASED BANKER

CHAPTER 1

Nobody Wants Your Products

Let's start with something that might sound a little harsh.

But if you're going to become a great banker, you need to hear it early, before the habits form, before the patterns set in, before you spend years optimizing for the wrong thing.

Nobody wants your products.

Not your checking account. Not your credit card. Not your auto loan. Not your home equity line. Nobody walks into a credit union on a Tuesday morning thinking: "I really hope someone sells me a financial product today."

That's not why people come in.

And once you truly understand why they do come in, everything about this job changes.

WHAT PEOPLE ARE ACTUALLY AFTER

Nobody wants a mortgage.

They want a home. A specific one, probably, maybe they've already driven past it a few times. A place to raise their kids, host holidays, finally have a yard. The mortgage is simply the mechanism that makes it possible. It's the bridge between where they are and where they want to be.

Nobody wants an auto loan.

They want the car. The reliable one that won't leave them stranded on the way to work. The bigger one now that the family has grown. Maybe something they're genuinely proud to drive. The loan is just the tool that gets them there.

Nobody wants a checking account.

They want their money to be safe and accessible. They want to pay bills without thinking twice. They want their paycheck to land somewhere dependable and their debit card to work every time. The account is just the container.

Here's the thing about containers and tools and bridges: nobody gets excited about them. People get excited about what they make possible.

A great banker understands that distinction instinctively. Every product they offer is in service of something the member is trying to accomplish, a goal, a transition, a dream, a problem they need to solve. The product is never the point. The person's life is the point.

Products are tools. Goals are what matter.

THE STORY BEHIND THE NUMBERS

There's a line I keep coming back to, one that captures the heart of this work better than anything else I've found:

> *Every financial decision lives inside a human story.*

Think about what that means for a moment.

The member applying for an auto loan isn't just a credit score and a debt-to-income ratio. She's a nurse who works night shifts and whose car broke down twice last month, and she's terrified of being stranded at 2 a.m.

on the way home from the hospital. The mortgage application isn't just a set of financials. It's a couple who have been renting for eleven years and are finally, nervously, ready to try.

The numbers are real and they matter. But behind every set of numbers is a person with a reason. A situation. A hope or a worry that brought them through the door.

When you see only the transcription, you miss the story.

And when you miss the story, you miss the opportunity to actually help.

THE MISTAKE MOST BANKERS MAKE

Most bankers start their careers focused on products. That's not a criticism, it's what they're trained to do. They memorize features, learn the rate sheets, study the promotions. They're taught to look for opportunities to offer something.

And so every conversation starts to feel like a search for the right moment to ask:

"Would you like to apply for that today?"

Members feel this almost immediately. They can sense when the conversation is oriented around your goals rather than theirs. And when people feel like they're being sold to, something closes. They answer questions quickly and briefly. They finish the transaction. They thank you and leave.

And the relationship never starts, because a relationship requires both people to be on the same side of the table, and the moment a member feels like they're being managed toward a product, they stop being a person in a conversation and become a target.

That's not what you want. And honestly, it's probably not what most bankers want either. Most people who go to work at a credit union did so because they wanted to help people with their finances. The product pressure comes later, and it can quietly reshape how the job feels.

This book is about reshaping it back.

A TALE OF TWO CONVERSATIONS

A member sits down and says: "I'm thinking about buying a car."

The average banker hears that and immediately thinks: auto loan. So they respond:

> *"We have some great rates right now. What vehicle are you looking at?"*

That's not wrong, exactly. But it skips something important.

A different banker hears the same thing and responds:

> *"That's exciting. What kind of car are you thinking about?"*

Small difference in words. Enormous difference in what happens next.

Now the member starts talking. Maybe the old car has been in the shop three times this year and he's finally had enough. Maybe his second child just arrived and the sedan suddenly feels too small. Maybe he commutes forty-five minutes each way and reliability has become non-negotiable.

Now the banker knows the story. And once you know the story, helping becomes natural. The right loan term, the right payment range, the right conversation about what makes sense, all of it becomes easier when you understand what the member is actually trying to solve.

The first banker got a transaction.

The second banker started a relationship.

WHY CURIOSITY IS THE REAL SKILL

Most new bankers assume the job is about product knowledge. Know your rates, know your features, know your promotions. And yes, that knowledge matters.

But it's not what separates average bankers from great ones.

What separates them is curiosity.

The willingness to ask before answering. To slow the conversation down just enough to understand the person before recommending the solution. To be genuinely interested in what the member is trying to accomplish, not because it's a technique, but because the work is more interesting and more satisfying when you understand the full picture.

When you're genuinely curious about the people sitting across from you, something happens. They relax. They open up. They tell you things they might not have planned to say. They share the real situation instead of just the stated request.

And that's when banking stops being transactional and starts being something worth doing.

THE CREDIT UNION DIFFERENCE

Here's something worth holding onto, especially early in your career.

Credit unions were built around a different idea than most financial institutions. Not customers, members. That word isn't an accident. It reflects a founding conviction: that the people who walk through the door deserve someone who is genuinely on their side. Someone looking out for their financial well-being, not just their transaction volume.

That's a meaningful advantage, if you choose to use it.

When you approach your role as a guide rather than a salesperson, members notice almost immediately. The conversation feels different. The dynamic shifts. They lean in instead of leaning back. They start asking questions they weren't sure it was okay to ask.

Because what they want, what most people want when they're trying to make an important financial decision, is someone they can trust to tell them the truth. Not someone trying to close them on something. Someone actually trying to help.

That's the role. And in a credit union, it fits.

THE QUESTION TO KEEP IN MIND

As you move through the chapters ahead, I want you to carry one question with you into every member interaction:

Am I talking about my products, or their goals?

It's a simple test. But it's reliable. When the conversation is centered on what you're offering, something is usually missing. When the conversation is centered on what the member is trying to accomplish, you're usually on the right track.

The best bankers ask this question instinctively, not because they were told to, but because they're genuinely more interested in the member's goals than in the product. That interest is what members feel. It's what makes them come back.

It's also what makes the work feel like something more than a series of transactions.

People don't come to a credit union looking for financial products.

They come looking for help.

The banker who learns how to provide that help, who listens before recommending, who asks before answering, who sees the human story behind every financial decision, will build something far more valuable than a sale.

They will build trust.

And trust, over time, builds everything else.

CHAPTER 2

Banker Truths

If you spend enough time in a credit union branch, you start to notice something.

Certain bankers just seem to connect with people.

Members gravitate toward them. Regulars come in and ask for them specifically, even when another banker is free. New members who had a single good experience find reasons to come back and find that same person. These bankers aren't necessarily the loudest in the room or the most polished. They're not always the most senior. But something about the way they work creates a kind of pull.

It's easy to assume the difference is personality. That some people are just naturally better with other people, and that's that.

But watch long enough and you'll see it's something else. It's not charisma. It's not a script. It's a set of convictions, about what the job actually is, about what members actually need, about what it means to help someone rather than just serve them.

These convictions tend to operate quietly, beneath the surface of every conversation. Most of the bankers who hold them couldn't always articulate them directly. They just know that some approaches feel right and others don't. Over years of practice, these convictions have shaped how they listen, how they ask questions, how they respond when a member is struggling, and how they stay patient when the conversation takes longer than the lobby pace demands.

I call them Banker Truths.

They're not complicated. But they change the way you see the job. And once you see the job this way, it's hard to unsee it.

BANKER TRUTH #1

Nobody Wants Your Products

We started here in the last chapter because it's the foundation everything else rests on.

Members don't want loans. They want homes, reliable transportation, a way to handle an unexpected expense without it becoming a crisis. They don't want checking accounts. They want their money to be safe, accessible, and easy to manage. They don't want credit cards. They want the convenience of not carrying cash, or the ability to handle something now and pay it off over time.

The product is the tool. The goal is what matters.

Great bankers never lose sight of that distinction. When a member sits down, the first question running through a great banker's mind isn't, which product fits here, it's, what is this person trying to accomplish? Everything else follows from that.

BANKER TRUTH #2

Curiosity Beats Persuasion

You don't need to convince people to work with you.

You need to understand them.

There's a version of banking that treats every conversation as a persuasion challenge, how do I move this person from where they are to where I need them to be? But that framing puts you and the member on opposite sides. And members can feel it. The conversation gets guarded. They answer questions with the minimum required. They're waiting for the pitch.

Curiosity works differently. When you ask genuine questions, and listen to the answers, something shifts. The member stops being a prospect and starts being a person. They share more than you asked for. They tell you the real story behind the stated request. And that story is almost always where the real opportunity to help lives.

Curiosity opens doors that persuasion never will. Not because it's a better technique, but because it changes the nature of the interaction entirely.

BANKER TRUTH #3

Advice Creates Loyalty

A product can open an account.

But advice builds a relationship.

There's a difference between a member who bought something from you and a member who was helped by you. The first one may come back when they need another product. The second one comes back before they've decided what they need, because they want to think it through with someone they trust first.

That's what advice creates. Not just a satisfied customer, but a member who has experienced what it feels like to have a banker genuinely on their side. That experience is rare enough that people remember it. They tell their spouses about it. They mention it to friends who are looking for a new bank.

Advice is the thing that turns a transaction into a relationship. And relationships, over time, are the whole job.

BANKER TRUTH #4

Members Remember How You Helped Them, Not What You Sold Them

Five years from now, a member will not remember the interest rate on their auto loan.

They will not remember the exact term, or which checking account tier they were in, or what the promotional rate was when they opened their savings account.

But they will remember the banker who took the time to look at their full financial picture before recommending a loan amount. They will remember the banker who explained the difference between two options without making them feel foolish for not already knowing. They will remember the banker who said: "Let's make sure this payment actually fits comfortably before we move forward."

People remember how an experience felt far longer than they remember its details. And the feeling that someone was genuinely trying to help them, not just complete a transaction, stays with people for years.

That's what you're building, every time you slow down long enough to actually help.

BANKER TRUTH #5

Listening Is the Skill Nobody Talks About

Most people are not used to being truly listened to. Especially when it comes to money.

Money is personal. It's tied up with self-worth and anxiety and hope and embarrassment in ways that most other topics aren't. Many members walk into a branch carrying more than they show, a worry they haven't named, a situation they're not sure how to explain, a decision that has been weighing on them for weeks.

Most bankers listen long enough to identify the product. Great bankers listen long enough to understand the person.

The difference is audible. When someone is listened to deeply, they open up in ways they didn't plan to. They share the context. They ask the questions they were afraid to ask. They stop managing the conversation and start having it.

And when a member leaves a conversation feeling genuinely heard, often for the first time in a financial setting, they remember who made that possible.

BANKER TRUTH #6

Every Financial Decision Lives Inside a Human Story

> *Behind every loan application is a reason it exists.*

Behind every account opening is a situation that prompted it. A young couple finally ready to stop renting. A parent who just agreed to help an adult child get back on their feet. A member who had something go wrong, a job loss, a medical bill, a divorce, and is quietly trying to rebuild.

The numbers on the screen tell you the financial picture. The conversation tells you the human one.

Both matter. But the human story is where you find out how to actually help. It's where you learn what success looks like from the member's perspective, what their real constraints are, what they're most worried about. Without it, you're making recommendations based on incomplete information.

When you understand the story, the right solution usually becomes obvious. When you skip it, you're guessing.

BANKER TRUTH #7

Transactions Are Openings, Not Endpoints

A deposit. A withdrawal. A question about a debit card charge. A replacement card.

These feel routine because they are routine, until you start treating them as the beginning of a conversation rather than the whole of it.

One follow-up question changes everything.

"That's a nice deposit, anything exciting going on?"

Or: "Is there anything else financially you've been thinking about lately?" Or simply: "How are things going?"

Sometimes nothing comes of it. The member smiles, answers briefly, and moves on. That's fine.

But sometimes the question opens a door. The member mentions something they've been wondering about. A life event surfaces. A financial situation that needed attention was just waiting for someone to ask.

Great bankers have trained themselves to see every transaction as a small window into a member's financial life. They look through it. Not every time. But often enough that they catch the moments worth catching.

BANKER TRUTH #8

Simplicity Is a Form of Respect

Financial language can be quietly alienating.

APR. Amortization. Debt-to-income ratio. Equity. Liquidity. Most members have heard these terms. Few of them could define them precisely. And in a conversation with a banker, many won't ask, because admitting you don't understand something about money can feel embarrassing.

So they nod. They sign. They leave with a product they may not fully understand, and the quiet unease of a decision they're not entirely sure about.

Great bankers translate. They take the technical language of finance and turn it into plain speech. Not because they think members aren't capable, but because clarity is a courtesy, and confidence grows when people actually understand what they're doing with their money.

When a member leaves a conversation feeling like they understand their own financial situation better than when they arrived, that's not a small thing. That's the job done well.

BANKER TRUTH #9

Trust Is Built in Small Moments

Trust doesn't arrive in a single conversation. It accumulates.

It grows in the small moments that most people don't think to track. Remembering a member's name the second time they come in. Following up on something they mentioned last visit, "How did that move go?" Taking an extra two minutes to explain something clearly instead of rushing to the next person in line. Saying "I don't know, but let me find out" instead of guessing.

None of these moments feel significant on their own. But members notice them. They add up. And over time, they create something that no single impressive conversation could build on its own: the sense that someone at the credit union actually knows them, and actually cares.

That's a rare thing in financial services. It's worth being intentional about.

BANKER TRUTH #10

The Best Bankers Ask Better Questions

Average bankers have good answers.

Great bankers have good questions.

The distinction matters because the best answer in the world is still just a guess if you don't understand the situation. A question, asked well, gives you the information you need to actually help. It also does something else, it signals to the member that you're interested in their situation, not just your solution.

The questions don't need to be elaborate. Some of the most useful ones are also the simplest.

What made you start thinking about this now?

What are you hoping to accomplish?

What would make you feel confident about this decision?

What concerns you most?

A good question opens the conversation. A great question opens the person. And once you understand the person, the right path forward usually becomes clear.

BANKER TRUTH #11

Sometimes the Best Advice Is "Not Yet"

This one takes confidence. But it might be the most important truth on this list.

Sometimes a member comes in ready to move forward on something that isn't quite right for them. The payment is higher than they realize. The timing is off. They're excited about a purchase that, once you look at the numbers together, is going to create real pressure in their budget.

The easy thing, the transactional thing, is to approve the loan, complete the application, and move on.

The harder thing, and the more valuable thing, is to say: "Let's make sure this feels right before we go further. Here's what I'm seeing."

When you help someone avoid a financial mistake, you earn something a sale can never buy. You earn credibility. The member learns, in a concrete way, that you are genuinely on their side, that your job, as you understand it, is to help them make a good decision, not just to process their paperwork.

Those moments build the deepest trust of all.

BANKER TRUTH #12

When You Help People, They Come Back

This is where all the other truths converge.

Members who feel genuinely helped don't just return. They return with more of their financial life. They bring their spouses in for a joint account, their adult children for a first loan, their friends who just moved to the area and are looking for somewhere to bank.

They become a source of referrals, not because you asked, but because when someone asks them "where do you bank?" they don't just name the institution. They name the person.

Your reputation doesn't grow from the products you moved. It grows from the people you helped, and from how clearly they remember feeling helped.

That's the long game in banking. And it's the one worth playing.

The Truth Behind the Truths

Read back through these twelve and you'll notice they all point toward the same thing.

People before products. Curiosity before conclusions. Advice before answers. Understanding before solutions.

That's the discipline. And it doesn't require a particular personality or a gift for sales or an unusual ability to charm strangers. It requires something more fundamental: the decision to show up to every conversation genuinely interested in the person across the desk and what they're trying to accomplish.

When that becomes the habit, when it stops being something you remind yourself to do and starts being simply how you work, something changes. Not just in how members experience you. In how you experience the job.

Because banking, practiced this way, isn't a series of transactions.

It's a series of relationships. And relationships, built slowly, one honest conversation at a time, are what make a career in this work worth having.

In the next chapter, we'll put a framework to all of this. It's called the Advice-Based Banker Pyramid, and it shows exactly how these truths play out in a real conversation, from the first question to the right solution.

CHAPTER 3

The Advice-Based Banker Pyramid

There's a pattern that shows up in almost every credit union branch, in almost every banker's early career, and it's worth naming directly before we go any further.

When a member mentions something, a car, a home, a savings goal, the banker's mind goes immediately to the product. Not out of laziness or indifference. Out of training. Out of the genuine desire to be helpful and to demonstrate knowledge. The member says "home" and the banker thinks "mortgage." The member says "car" and the banker thinks "auto loan." The member says "I want to save more" and the banker reaches for the savings account brochure.

It feels like helping. And in a narrow sense, it is.

But there's a problem with starting there, and it's more significant than it first appears.

When you start with the product, you're guessing.

You're guessing what the member actually needs. You're guessing what matters most to them. You're guessing what kind of solution will actually fit their life. And sometimes you guess right, the member did want exactly what you offered, and the transaction closes cleanly.

But you never find out what you missed. You never learn that the member asking about a car loan is actually worried about overextending herself. Or that the member who came in about savings has a specific goal, a wedding, a trip, a down payment, that would completely change which product made the most sense. Or that the member who nodded through the mortgage presentation went home that night and told his wife: "I'm still not sure we're ready."

The guessing problem is invisible when you're guessing correctly. It only surfaces in the relationships that never deepen, the members who don't come back, the trust that never quite forms.

Great bankers solve this problem not by knowing more products, but by asking more questions, and by understanding that the conversation has a natural order that, when followed, leads consistently to better outcomes for the member and a stronger relationship for the banker.

That order is what I call **The Advice-Based Banker Pyramid**.

The Pyramid

Picture four levels, stacked from bottom to top.

The bottom level is the widest, it's the foundation. The top level is the narrowest, where the specific solution lives. Every level rests on the one below it. Skip a level and the whole thing becomes unstable.

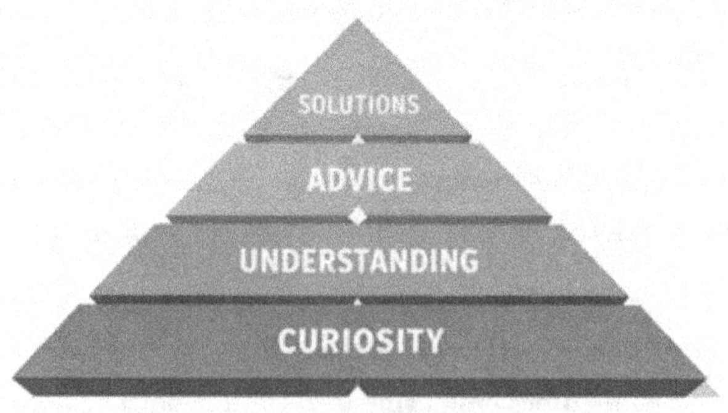

Most bankers work from the top down. They start with solutions and then try to build a case for them. The Advice-Based Banker Pyramid works from the bottom up. You earn the right to recommend a solution by first doing the work of understanding the person who needs one.

Here's what each level actually looks like in a real conversation.

Level 1: Curiosity

Curiosity is the foundation. Not just as a concept, as a practice. As the first thing you do when a member sits down across from you, before you've made any assumptions about what they need or what product might fit.

Curiosity sounds like questions. Simple ones, asked with genuine interest.

What brings you in today?

What made you start thinking about this?

What are you hoping to figure out?

These questions do something that product presentations cannot: they invite the member into the conversation as a participant rather than an audience. They signal, immediately and unmistakably, that you are here to understand their situation, not to deliver a pitch.

They also give you information you cannot get any other way. The story behind the request. The context that changes everything. The detail that tells you which direction to actually go.

One thing worth noting about curiosity: it has to be genuine. Members can tell the difference between a banker who is asking questions to check a box and one who is actually interested in the answers. The first kind creates guarded, minimal responses. The second kind opens the conversation up in ways that are often surprising, and consistently useful.

Curiosity is the level that everything else is built on. Rush past it, and you're back to guessing.

Level 2: Understanding

Curiosity gathers the story. Understanding makes sense of it.

This is the level where you slow down and actually process what you've heard. Where you move from "what did the member say?" to "what does the member actually need?" Those are often different things, and the gap between them is where great bankers earn their value.

A member says she's looking for an auto loan. Curiosity reveals that her car has broken down twice in the past two months. Understanding reveals something more specific: that what she really needs isn't just any car loan, she needs a reliable vehicle as quickly as possible, and she's anxious about taking on more monthly payment than she can manage. Her priority isn't the lowest rate. It's the right car at a payment that won't keep her up at night.

Now you're not guessing anymore. You know what success looks like from her perspective. You know what she's worried about. You know what would actually help.

Understanding is also the level where you notice what members don't say. The hesitation before they answer a question. The qualifier that suggests they're not quite as sure as they're presenting. The detail that doesn't quite add up. Part of understanding is reading the full picture, not just the stated request, but the situation surrounding it.

When you've reached genuine understanding, you'll often feel it. The conversation has a different quality. The member is more engaged. You have a clear sense of the problem you're actually trying to solve. And you're ready to do something most bankers skip entirely.

Level 3: Advice

This is the level that separates the banker members remember from the banker they forget.

Advice is not selling. It is not presenting options in a way designed to move the member toward a particular outcome. It is not enthusiastic description of product features. Advice is genuinely helping someone think through a decision, offering your perspective, your experience, your honest assessment of their situation, in service of helping them make a better choice.

It sounds like this:

> *Here's something worth considering before you decide.*
>
> *In my experience, members in a similar situation have often found that…*
>
> *Let me show you two different ways to approach this, and you can tell me which feels right.*
>
> *I want to make sure you've thought about this part before we move forward.*

That last one is especially important. Advice sometimes means flagging something the member hasn't considered. A payment that's higher than it looks when you factor in their other expenses. A loan term that seems attractive now but creates problems later. A decision that might make more sense in six months than today.

When you offer that kind of advice, honest, specific, genuinely in the member's interest, something happens in the room. The dynamic changes. The member can feel that you're on their side. That you're not trying to close a transaction. That your goal and their goal are actually the same: a decision they'll feel good about.

Trust, which is slow to build and easy to lose, accelerates at this level more than any other.

Only after you've offered genuine advice are you ready to move to the top of the pyramid.

Level 4: Solutions

This is where the product enters the conversation.

Notice where it enters: last. After curiosity, after understanding, after advice. Not because products are unimportant, they're the practical tools that make financial goals possible, but because a product recommendation lands completely differently when it arrives at the right moment.

When a member has been heard, when their situation has been understood, when they've received honest advice that helped them think clearly, and then a specific solution is recommended, it doesn't feel like a sale. It feels like the natural conclusion of a conversation that was always about helping them.

The mortgage doesn't feel like a financial instrument. It feels like the path to the home they've been describing. The auto loan doesn't feel like a credit decision. It feels like the answer to the reliability problem they just walked you through. The savings account doesn't feel like a product. It feels like the container for the goal they just clarified.

That's the difference the pyramid makes. Same products. Entirely different experience of receiving them.

Why the Order Is Everything

Most bankers, most of the time, work the pyramid upside down, and they often don't realize it because the transactions still close. The applications get submitted. The loans get approved. The accounts get opened. The numbers on the board move.

But something is missing. And members feel it even when they can't name it. The conversation felt efficient but not warm. Helpful in a technical sense but not in the way that makes you want to go back to the same person. The banker knew their products but didn't seem particularly curious about the person buying them.

The flipped pyramid produces transactions. ***The right-side-up pyramid produces relationships.***

And relationships, members who return, who refer others, who bring more of their financial life to the same person over time, are what a meaningful career in banking is built on.

The Pyramid in Practice

Here's what this looks like in a real interaction. Not an idealized version, a realistic one.

A member sits down on a Wednesday afternoon and says he's thinking about refinancing his mortgage. He's read something online about rates and wondered if it made sense.

A banker working from the top of the pyramid reaches for the rate sheet. Starts talking about current rates, points, closing costs. It's accurate. It's relevant. But it skips something.

A banker working from the bottom starts with curiosity.

What made you start thinking about refinancing now?

The member explains: he got a raise last year, his budget has loosened up, and he's been wondering if he could pay the house off faster without it hurting too much each month.

Now understanding. The banker takes a moment. This member isn't trying to lower his monthly payment, he's trying to shorten his timeline. Those are opposite strategies. A lower rate on a 30-year loan would reduce his payment but extend his term. What he actually needs to think about is a 15-year option, or making extra principal payments on his existing loan.

Now advice.

> *Let me show you two different scenarios and explain the trade-offs between them. One gets you to paid-off faster. The other keeps your payment flexible. Here's what each one looks like over time.*

Now the member is engaged. He leans forward. He asks questions. He's not passively receiving information, he's actively working through a decision with someone who is clearly trying to help him get it right.

The solution arrives when it's ready. And when it does, it fits.

That's the pyramid working the way it's designed to.

A Simple Thing to Remember

The framework has four levels. But if you want a single thought to carry into every conversation, it's this:

> ***Earn the right to recommend.***

Earn it by being curious. Earn it by understanding. Earn it by offering honest advice. When you've done those things, when the member feels heard and helped and clear, the solution you recommend will land the way it's supposed to.

Not as a product. As the answer to a question they actually had.

In the next chapter, we'll take the pyramid and turn it into a step-by-step conversation framework called the GUIDE Model, a practical tool you can use in every member interaction, starting tomorrow

CHAPTER 4

From Salesperson to Guide

Early in their careers, most bankers feel a tension they don't quite have words for.

On one side: the reason they took the job. They wanted to help people with their finances. They liked the idea of sitting across from someone navigating an important decision and actually being useful. Maybe they had a personal experience, a banker who helped their family through something, that showed them what the job could be at its best.

On the other side: the reality of how performance gets measured. Products opened. Loans approved. Accounts added. A scoreboard on the wall or a number on a spreadsheet that tells everyone, including you, how you're doing.

And so the tension forms. Because helping people and selling products are not the same thing. They can overlap. They often do. But they're not the same. And when you're measured primarily on the second, it quietly reshapes how you approach the first.

What gets lost, usually without anyone naming it, is the role.

Not the job title. The role. The thing that makes the work meaningful, and the thing that, paradoxically, also drives the best long-term results.

The role of a guide.

Salesperson vs. Guide

The distinction sounds simple. But it runs deeper than it might first appear.

A salesperson starts with the product and works backward toward the customer. Their job is to match what they have to what the customer might want, and to make the case for it compellingly. This isn't cynical, salespeople can be genuinely helpful and genuinely good at what they do. But the orientation is product-first. The product is the anchor.

A guide starts with the person and works forward toward the solution. Their job is to understand where someone is trying to go and help them find the best path to get there. The product, if it's the right one, arrives at the end of that process, not at the beginning.

The difference in the member's experience is immediate and unmistakable.

When someone feels sold to, they become careful. They give shorter answers. They're on guard for the pitch. They stop sharing the full picture of their situation because they sense that sharing it might be used to move them somewhere they haven't decided to go.

When someone feels guided, something opens. They talk more freely. They ask questions they weren't sure it was okay to ask. They share the context, the real story, because the conversation feels safe. Because the person across the desk seems genuinely interested in helping them figure something out, not in closing them on something.

That's the environment in which trust forms. And trust, in banking, is everything.

What a Guide Actually Does

The analogy I find most useful is a hiking guide.

A hiking guide doesn't start by handing you a trail map and pointing you toward the most popular route. They start by asking questions. What's your experience level? How long do you have? What are you hoping to see, the summit, the waterfall, the quiet stretch of forest? Are your knees okay with steep terrain?

Only after they understand who you are and what you're looking for do they say: here's the path that makes the most sense for you.

And notice something important about that moment. When the recommendation comes after the questions, you trust it. You don't feel like you're being directed toward the path that's easiest for the guide, or the one that's most popular. You feel like this person actually listened to what you said and found the option that fits your specific situation.

That's the experience members have when a banker guides instead of sells.

The recommendation feels earned. It feels like it came from somewhere real, from an actual understanding of their situation, rather than from a menu of available options.

The GUIDE Model

To make this concrete and practical, something you can actually use in a real conversation, starting tomorrow, here is a simple five-step framework.

The GUIDE Model. Each letter is a step. Together they describe the natural shape of a conversation that builds trust.

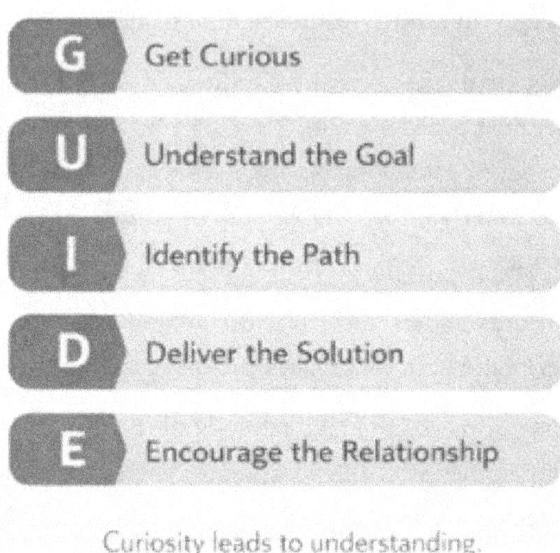

G, Get Curious

This is where the conversation starts. Not with products, not with applications, not with paperwork, with questions.

What brings you in today?

What made you start thinking about this?

What are you hoping to figure out?

These questions do two things simultaneously. They gather information you can't get any other way, and they signal to the member, immediately, unmistakably, that you're interested in their situation, not just their transaction.

Getting curious isn't a technique you perform. It's an orientation you bring. The best way to ask good questions is to actually care about the answers. And if you let yourself be genuinely curious about the people who sit across from you, about their lives, their goals, their worries, the questions come naturally.

One practical note: in a busy branch, getting curious can feel like a luxury. The line is long, the lobby is full, the afternoon is packed. The pressure to move quickly is real. But often the difference between a transactional interaction and a meaningful one is a single question, one that takes thirty seconds to ask but changes the entire shape of what follows.

The return on curiosity is almost always worth the investment.

U, Understand the Goal

Once the conversation begins, your job shifts from asking to listening, and from listening to understanding.

This is the step where you move past the stated request and toward the actual goal. As we talked about in Chapter 1, those are often different things. The stated request is the surface. The goal is what the member is really trying to accomplish.

A member who says "I want to apply for a personal loan" might be trying to consolidate debt that's been stressing her out for two years. A member who says "I need to open a savings account" might be saving for a down payment and wondering whether he's on track. A member who says "I'm looking for information about auto loans" might be replacing a car that finally gave out and is anxious about the timing.

Understanding the goal means staying curious long enough to find out what's actually going on. Asking a follow-up question when the first answer sounds incomplete. Noticing the detail that doesn't quite fit and gently exploring it.

When you understand the goal, the real one, not just the stated one, you've done something most financial service interactions never do: you've treated the member as a person with a situation, rather than a customer with a request.

I, Identify the Path

Now advice enters the conversation.

This is the step where your experience and knowledge actually become valuable, not as a catalog of products to present, but as a perspective to offer. You've heard the member's situation. You understand what they're trying to accomplish and what they're worried about. Now you help them think through what comes next.

> *Here are a couple of ways to approach this, let me walk you through the trade-offs.*
>
> *Given what you've told me, here's what I'd want you to consider before deciding.*
>
> *Some members in a similar situation have found that starting here actually makes the next step easier.*

Notice the orientation. You're not pitching. You're thinking alongside the member. You're using what you know, about products, about financial decisions, about what tends to work and what tends to create problems, to help them see their options more clearly.

This is also the step where you say the harder things, when they need to be said. The payment that's going to feel bigger than they think. The timing that's not quite right. The alternative they hadn't considered that might serve them better. Advice that's always comfortable isn't really advice, it's just agreement. Real guidance sometimes means offering a perspective the member didn't expect, in service of helping them make a better decision.

D, Deliver the Solution

Now, and only now, does the product enter the conversation.

By the time you arrive here, something has shifted. The member has been heard. Their goal is clear. They've thought through their options with someone who was genuinely trying to help. The recommendation you're about to make connects directly to everything they just shared.

In that context, the product doesn't feel like a product. It feels like the answer.

The auto loan is the path to the reliable truck he needs before winter. The savings account is the structure that gets her to the down payment by next spring. The debt consolidation loan is the way out of the cycle that's been weighing on him for longer than he wants to admit.

When products arrive this way, as solutions to understood problems, recommended by someone the member has come to trust in the span of a single conversation, they land completely differently than when they're the first thing out of the banker's mouth. The member doesn't feel sold to. They feel helped.

E, Encourage the Relationship

This is the step most bankers skip, and it's a significant missed opportunity.

The conversation is winding down. The solution has been delivered. Everything is in order. The natural instinct is to wrap up, hand over the paperwork, and thank the member for coming in.

Instead, pause for a moment. And say something like:

> *If you ever want to talk through a financial decision before you make it, I'm happy to be a sounding board. That's what I'm here for.*

If anything comes up and you want another set of eyes on it, just reach out.

These are small moments. They take fifteen seconds. But they plant an idea in the member's mind that has real long-term value: that you are available, that you're interested in their financial life beyond this transaction, and that coming back to you is an option when the next decision arrives.

The E step is how individual transactions become ongoing relationships. It's the moment where you explicitly signal that you want to be someone the member returns to, not just someone they dealt with once.

Why the GUIDE Model Works

The model works because it follows the natural shape of how trust forms between people.

First, someone has to feel heard. Then understood. Then genuinely helped. Then, and only then, do they accept a recommendation with real confidence.

Most sales approaches try to skip directly to the recommendation. And sometimes the transaction closes anyway, because the member needed what was offered and it was available. But the trust doesn't form. The relationship doesn't start. The member walks out having gotten what they asked for, but not feeling particularly compelled to come back to the same person for the next thing.

The GUIDE model doesn't shortcut any of these steps. It respects the order. And the result is not just a completed transaction, it's a member who felt the difference.

The Identity Shift

There's something deeper here than a conversation model, and it's worth naming directly.

The shift from salesperson to guide isn't just a change in technique. It's a change in how you see your role. In what you're actually optimizing for when you sit down with a member. In what you consider a successful interaction.

A salesperson measures success by the close. Did the product get offered? Did the member say yes?

A guide measures success by the outcome. Does the member understand their decision? Do they feel confident about it? Is this the right solution for their actual situation?

When you make that shift, when you start measuring your interactions by the quality of guidance rather than the number of products, something changes in how the work feels. It becomes more interesting. More engaging. More like the job you probably thought it would be when you started.

And it produces better results. Not immediately, necessarily. But over time, as members return and refer others and bring more of their financial life to someone they trust, the metrics catch up to the approach.

> ***The guide outperforms the salesperson. Every time, over the long run.***

In the next chapter, we'll look at the five types of conversations that show up in every branch, every day, and how to guide each one well.

PART II

THE CONVERSTAION THAT CHANGED EVERYTHING

CHAPTER 5

The Five Conversations Every Banker Must Master

Here's something that takes a little while to see, but once you see it you can't unsee it.

Members walk into a credit union branch for all kinds of reasons. Different ages, different situations, different requests. But underneath that variety, the conversations tend to fall into a handful of recognizable shapes, five of them, to be specific. The same types of moments, driven by the same kinds of things happening in people's lives, showing up day after day in every branch.

Most bankers work for years without consciously recognizing this. They approach each interaction fresh, without a framework for what kind of conversation they're actually in. That's not wrong, every member deserves to be treated as an individual. But there's a real advantage in being able to recognize the pattern quickly, because each type of conversation calls for something slightly different from the banker. Different questions to lead with. Different things to listen for. A different sense of what success looks like.

The five conversations are not a script. They're a map. A way of reading what's actually happening in the interaction so you can show up in it the right way.

Here's what they look like.

CONVERSATION 1

The Goal Conversation

This is the most common conversation in banking, and the one most frequently reduced to a transaction when it doesn't have to be.

Members almost never walk in and say: "I have a financial goal I'd like to discuss." What they say is:

I want to apply for a loan.

I need to open a savings account.

I'm looking into credit cards.

These are requests. They're specific, action-oriented, and they tell you what the member wants to do. But they don't tell you why. And the why is almost always the more important piece.

Behind the loan application is something the loan is supposed to make possible. Behind the savings account is a number the member is trying to reach, or a feeling of security they're trying to create. Behind the credit card question is a purchase, a habit, a plan, something.

Your job in the Goal Conversation is not to process the request. It's to understand what's driving it.

One question is usually enough to open it up.

What are you hoping to accomplish?

What happens next is almost always more interesting than what the member said when they sat down. They start talking about the home they've been saving toward for three years. The debt they've been carrying since a difficult stretch that's finally starting to feel manageable. The trip they've been promising their kids. The business idea that's been sitting in the back of their mind.

Now you're not processing a request. You're helping someone move toward something that matters to them. That's a completely different conversation, and it produces a completely different outcome.

CONVERSATION 2

The Life Moment Conversation

Financial decisions don't happen in a vacuum. They happen in the middle of people's lives, triggered by the same events that shape everything else: new jobs, new relationships, new babies, new homes, health scares, losses, retirements, departures.

The Life Moment Conversation usually doesn't announce itself. It arrives tucked inside a sentence that sounds like small talk.

We're expecting our first, due in April.

My mom passed away last month. I'm handling some of her accounts.

I just accepted a new position, I start in two weeks.

My son is getting married in the fall.

Most bankers hear these comments and respond with warmth, congratulations or I'm so sorry, and then return to the transaction at hand. Which is kind. But it misses something.

Life changes almost always carry financial implications. The new baby means new expenses, possibly a change in income, and eventually college to think about. The inherited accounts mean decisions about where assets go. The new job might mean a different income, a new city, or a 401(k) that needs a home. The wedding is months of expenses the family may or may not have planned for.

The member who mentions these things isn't necessarily asking for financial guidance. But they're often open to it, especially when the banker asks the right question.

> *That's a big transition. How are you feeling about the financial side of everything?*
>
> *I'm sorry for your loss. If there's anything I can help you navigate on the financial side, I'm happy to sit down with you.*
>
> *Congratulations on the new role. Are there any financial adjustments you're thinking through with the change?*

These questions are gentle. They leave the door open without pushing anyone through it. But they do something important: they signal that you're paying attention to the member's life, not just their account balance. And for members navigating real transitions, that signal matters.

The Life Moment Conversation is often where the deepest and most durable banking relationships begin.

CONVERSATION 3

The Money Stress Conversation

Not everyone who walks into a branch is having a good day financially.

Some members come in carrying real stress. A card that was declined at the grocery store. An overdraft they didn't see coming. A loan payment that's become harder to make than it used to be. A balance on a credit card that crept up slowly and now feels out of control.

Money stress is different from other kinds of stress. It's personal in a way that's hard to explain. It touches on security and self-worth and the sense of having things under control. When that sense slips, the embarrassment can be as painful as the practical problem. Many members dealing with financial difficulty have spent days or weeks avoiding the conversation they're about to have with you.

That's the context in which they're sitting down across the desk.

The worst thing a banker can do in this moment is make the member feel worse about their situation. Rush to fix the problem without acknowledging the difficulty. Explain what went wrong in a way that sounds like a lecture. Let impatience show, even slightly.

The best thing a banker can do is slow down and make the member feel safe.

Let's take a look ***together*** *and figure out what's going on.*

That word, together, matters more than it might seem. It signals that you're not on opposite sides of the problem. You're trying to solve it as a team.

From there, if the moment feels right, one gentle question can open the real conversation.

Do you mind if I ask what's been going on more broadly? Sometimes there's a bigger picture that helps me figure out how to actually help.

Often the member will share more than they planned to. A job change that cut their income. Medical bills that arrived all at once. A period of things going sideways that they're still working through. And once you understand the real situation, you can offer something much more useful than a waived fee or a quick fix.

You can offer a path forward. A reorganization of accounts. A repayment plan. A realistic look at what's manageable and what options exist. The sense that someone understands what they're dealing with and is genuinely trying to help them improve it.

The practical help matters. But what the member will carry out of that branch is how they were treated. Whether they felt judged or supported. Whether they left a little lighter or a little heavier than when they walked in.

The Money Stress Conversation, handled well, is one of the most powerful trust-building moments in banking. Members remember who was kind to them when things were hard. And that memory lasts far longer than any product feature or interest rate.

CONVERSATION 4

The Big Decision Conversation

Sometimes a member comes in not to complete a transaction, but to think out loud.

They've been turning something over for a while. They have some information, maybe even a tentative plan. But they want a second perspective before they commit. They want someone who understands these decisions to help them see what they might be missing.

Should I pay off my car early or keep the cash in savings?

We're thinking about pulling from our home equity for a renovation, does that make sense?

I've been carrying this credit card balance for two years. Is a personal loan actually going to help me or just move the problem?

These are good questions. They're the questions of someone who's trying to make a thoughtful decision rather than a rushed one. And they deserve something better than a quick answer.

The instinct, for many bankers, is to respond with confidence. To be the expert. To give the member a clear direction so they leave feeling like they got something useful.

Resist it, at least initially.

The better move is to sit with the question for a moment. Ask a few things before offering anything.

What's making you lean one way right now?

What's your biggest concern about each option?

What does the right answer feel like for you, is it the one that saves the most money, or the one that simplifies things, or something else?

These questions do something that a direct answer can't: they help the member understand their own thinking. They surface the values and priorities that should be shaping the decision. And often, once those are visible, the right answer becomes obvious, not because the banker told the member what to do, but because the banker helped them see clearly enough to decide for themselves.

That's a profoundly different experience. The member doesn't leave with the banker's answer. They leave with their own answer, reached with help. That distinction matters to people. They feel more confident in a decision they understood and participated in than one they were simply directed toward.

And they remember who created that experience.

CONVERSATION 5

The Future Conversation

This is the rarest conversation in banking, and arguably the most valuable.

It's rare because almost nothing in the typical branch interaction prompts it. Members come in with needs. Bankers solve needs. The whole system is oriented toward the present: what's happening now, what's needed now, what can be resolved today.

The Future Conversation is different. It's not about a current need. It's about where the member is trying to go, and whether anyone is helping them think about how to get there.

Most members have financial goals. A home they want to own eventually. A retirement that feels more real than abstract. A child's education they're vaguely aware they should be saving for. A level of financial cushion that would let them sleep better at night. These goals exist in the background of their financial life, often unspoken, occasionally thought about, rarely planned for in any deliberate way.

No one has ever sat them down and simply asked.

> ***What financial goal would you love to accomplish in the next few years?***

That question is deceptively simple. But for many members, it's the first time anyone in a financial institution has expressed interest in their future rather than their current transaction. The response is often surprisingly candid, and often reveals both a real goal and a clear gap between where the member is and where they want to be.

Which is exactly where a banker becomes genuinely useful.

The Future Conversation doesn't require special products or complex planning tools. It requires curiosity and patience. The willingness to ask the question, listen to the answer, and then help the member think about what a first step might look like.

Sometimes that first step leads to something concrete: a savings account opened, an automatic transfer set up, a loan restructured to free up cash flow. Sometimes it's simply a plan outlined on paper. Sometimes it's just a conversation that plants a seed, a member who walks out thinking about their financial future in a slightly more deliberate way than when they walked in.

That's not a small thing. Helping someone connect their daily financial decisions to a longer-term goal is genuinely useful. It's the kind of help that most people never get from a financial institution, and the kind that, when they do get it, they don't forget.

Reading the Room

Recognizing which conversation you're in is a skill that develops with practice. It won't always be obvious. Sometimes a member comes in for one type of conversation and reveals another. Sometimes the Money Stress Conversation is hiding inside a Goal Conversation. Sometimes a Life Moment surfaces in the middle of a routine transaction.

The framework isn't a rigid sorting system. It's a lens, a way of staying attuned to what's actually happening in the interaction beneath the stated request.

Here are the signals to watch for.

A member who comes in energized, talking about something they want to do or build: that's usually a Goal Conversation. A member who mentions something changing in their life, a baby, a move, a retirement, a loss, has handed you the opening for a Life Moment Conversation. A member who comes in tense, speaking quickly, eyes slightly down: that's often Money Stress. A member who comes in with a question they've clearly been sitting on: that's the Big Decision Conversation. And a member who mentions something they hope for someday, almost apologetically, as if it's too far off to be worth discussing, is standing right at the entrance to the Future Conversation, waiting to be invited in.

You don't announce the framework. You just use it. Quietly, in the background, it shapes how you listen, what you ask next, and what kind of help you reach for.

That attentiveness, the sense that you're really paying attention, that you understand not just the transaction but the person, is what members feel when they leave a conversation thinking: that was different.

Different is what this book is about.

In the next chapter, we'll go deeper on the tool that makes all five conversations work: the art and practice of asking great questions.

CHAPTER 6

The Power of Great Questions

There's a skill that separates the bankers members remember from the ones they forget. It's not product knowledge. It's not closing technique. It's not years of experience, though experience helps.

It's the ability to ask a question that opens something up.

Most people in financial services are trained to have answers. To know the rates, know the products, know the features, know the process. And that knowledge matters, members need bankers who understand what they're talking about. But knowledge without curiosity is just a catalog. It tells you what's available. It doesn't tell you what's needed.

Questions are what bridge the gap between those two things. A well-placed question reveals the situation behind the request, the goal behind the product, the person behind the transaction. It turns a conversation where you're guessing into one where you actually know. And knowing, really knowing what a member is trying to accomplish and why, is what makes it possible to help them in a way that sticks.

The best bankers are not the ones with the most answers. They're the ones who know which question to ask next.

What Questions Actually Do

It's worth slowing down on this for a moment, because questions do more than just gather information.

When you ask a thoughtful question, the member experiences something before they even answer it. They experience being noticed. Being treated as someone with a situation that's worth understanding, not just a request to be processed. In most financial service interactions, that experience is genuinely rare, and it registers immediately.

Questions also slow the conversation down in a way that turns out to be useful. The instinct in a busy branch is to move quickly, to be efficient, to get to the point. But the point is often buried underneath the stated request, and it only surfaces if the conversation slows down long enough to find it. A question creates that space. It says: I'm not in a hurry to get past you. I'm interested in what you're actually dealing with.

And questions create clarity. Not just for you, for the member too. Many people walk into a branch without a fully formed picture of what they need. They have a sense of the problem, an instinct about a solution, a vague awareness that something needs to happen. A good question helps them articulate what they've only been thinking about loosely. And when members can articulate their situation clearly, when they understand it better themselves, the right path forward becomes visible to both of you.

This is what curiosity looks like in practice. It's not a mindset that lives in the abstract. It lives in the questions.

The Question Beneath the Question

Here's a pattern worth understanding, because it shows up constantly.

A member states a request. The request is real, they do want what they're asking for. But the request is sitting on top of something else: a goal, a worry, a situation that prompted the visit. The request is what the member knows how to say. The thing underneath it is what they actually need help with.

A member says: "I want to apply for a personal loan." The request is clear. But underneath it might be credit card debt that's been building for two years and is finally starting to feel unmanageable. Or a home repair that can't wait. Or a payment due on something they're embarrassed to name.

A member says: "I'm thinking about opening a savings account." Straightforward. But underneath it might be a down payment goal they've been working toward quietly, and they want to know if they're on track. Or a new job with better pay and a vague intention to finally start saving. Or a spouse who gave them an ultimatum about getting their finances in order.

You can't see what's underneath from the surface. You have to ask.

The question that reliably opens this up is also the simplest one.

> *What are you hoping to accomplish?*

Four words. But they do something that almost no other question does: they invite the member to talk about the outcome rather than the product. And once they're talking about outcomes, you're in a completely different conversation, one where you can actually help.

Questions in Practice: What They Sound Like

Questions don't need to be elaborate. The best ones usually aren't. They need to be genuine, well-timed, and pointed at the thing you actually want to understand.

Here's what that looks like across different situations.

WHEN A MEMBER IS WORKING TOWARD A GOAL

What are you hoping to accomplish with this?

What would success look like here for you?

Is there something specific you're working toward financially right now?

What made you start thinking about this now?

WHEN A MEMBER MENTIONS SOMETHING HAPPENING IN THEIR LIFE

That sounds like a big change, how are you thinking about the financial side of it?

What's coming up for you in the next year or so?

Has anything shifted in your finances recently?

WHEN A MEMBER SEEMS TO BE WEIGHING A DECISION

What options have you been looking at?

What's pulling you toward one direction over the other?

What's your biggest hesitation?

What would make you feel confident about this?

WHEN SOMETHING FEELS OFF

Do you mind if I ask what's been going on?

Is there anything on the financial side that's been worrying you?

What would make things feel simpler right now?

WHEN THE TRANSACTION MIGHT BE PART OF SOMETHING BIGGER

Is there anything else financially that's been on your mind lately?

Has anyone ever sat down with you to talk through your financial goals?

If you ever wanted a second set of eyes on a financial decision, would that be useful?

None of these questions require a script. They require curiosity, a genuine interest in the answer, which shapes how you ask and how you listen. When that's present, the exact phrasing matters less than the orientation behind it.

The Art of Listening to the Answer

Asking a good question is only half the skill. The other half is what you do with what you hear.

Many bankers ask questions but don't fully listen to the answers. They ask, then wait for their turn to talk. They hear the surface of what was said but miss the detail that changes everything. They take the first answer at face value without noticing the hesitation that came with it, or the qualifier that suggested something more.

Deep listening has a few specific qualities.

It's unhurried. The member can feel when a banker is waiting for them to finish rather than actually absorbing what they're saying. Slowing down, making full eye contact, not reaching for the keyboard, not glancing at the clock, signals that you're actually present.

It's curious about what's not said. People often circle around the most important thing before saying it directly. The member who says "things have been a little tight lately" may be describing a significant financial crisis. The one who says "I've been thinking about this for a while" may have a goal they've been afraid to say out loud. Follow the thread.

It follows up. The follow-up question is often more valuable than the original one, because it goes one level deeper. "What made that feel like the right move?" Or: "When you say tight, what does that look like?" Or simply: "Tell me more about that."

It doesn't rush toward the solution. There's a natural pull, once you've heard enough to identify a product that might help, to move toward it. That pull is worth resisting just a moment longer. Make sure you've heard the full picture before you reach for the answer.

You Only Need One

Looking at a full list of questions can feel overwhelming. It can start to feel like a performance, like you need to cycle through a sequence to demonstrate that you've asked enough.

That's not how it works.

In most conversations, one good question is enough to change everything. One question that catches the member off guard in the best possible way, that asks about something they weren't expecting to be asked about, can open up a conversation that neither of you planned to have. And that conversation is usually the most useful one.

The goal isn't to ask twenty questions. The goal is to ask the right one at the right moment. That takes practice, and it takes paying attention. But it doesn't take a script.

What it takes is genuine interest in the person sitting across from you. When that's present, the questions find themselves.

From Technique to Habit

Questions start out as something you remind yourself to ask. Then, with practice, they become something you ask naturally. And eventually, for the bankers who really internalize this, they stop feeling like questions at all. They feel like curiosity. Like the normal way of approaching another person's financial situation.

That shift is worth working toward. Because there's a meaningful difference between a banker who asks good questions because they were trained to and a banker who asks good questions because they're genuinely interested in what the member is trying to figure out. Members can tell the difference. The first kind feels like a process. The second kind feels like a person.

The habit of curiosity is what turns a skilled banker into a trusted one. And trusted is what this book is ultimately about, the kind of relationship where a member walks in, looks for you specifically, and says: "I wanted to talk to you before I decided anything."

That moment starts with a question.

In the next chapter, we'll look at how all of this plays out in the most ordinary moments of branch life, and why even the simplest transaction can be the beginning of something more.

CHAPTER 7

Turning Transactions Into Relationships

Stand in a credit union branch lobby for a morning and watch what happens.

A member comes in, handles something, leaves. Another comes in, handles something, leaves. The rhythm is steady. Deposits, withdrawals, debit card questions, loan payoff amounts, account changes. Each interaction is clean, professional, finished in a few minutes. From the outside, it looks like a well-run operation.

And it is. But something else is also happening, or could be, if you're paying attention.

Inside almost every one of those quick transactions is a small window into a member's life. A check that represents a life change. A question that hints at a decision being made. A comment dropped almost in passing that reveals something worth knowing. Most of these windows open and close in under a minute. Most of the time, nobody looks through them.

The bankers who build the strongest relationships have learned to look.

The Difference Between a Transaction and a Conversation

The distinction sounds simple, but it shapes everything.

A transaction is an exchange. Something is requested, something is provided, the interaction ends. Both parties were professional. The thing got done. Technically, a success.

A conversation is something else. It's two people actually connecting, even briefly, over something real. The member says something beyond the request. The banker responds to it. A moment of genuine human contact passes between them. And something sticks, even slightly, that wasn't there before.

The distance between a transaction and a conversation is often a single question.

A member comes in to deposit a check. The transaction version of this interaction takes ninety seconds.

"How would you like that deposited?"

"Into checking."

"Anything else today?"

"No thanks."

"Have a great day."

Done. Correct. Forgettable.

Now the conversation version. The banker processes the deposit the same way, efficiently, professionally. But before the member turns to leave, she asks one more thing.

"That's a nice deposit. Anything exciting going on?"

Maybe the member laughs and says it's a bonus from work. Maybe he mentions he just sold his boat. Maybe she says it's from a side project she's been working on. Whatever the answer, the conversation has opened. There's something to respond to. A thread to follow.

"A bonus, that's great. Busy year?"

Or: "What are you going to do with it?"

Or simply: "Good timing?"

Now the banker knows something. And the member knows something too, that this isn't just someone processing their paperwork. It's someone who noticed, and was curious, and took fifteen seconds to make the interaction feel like more than a task.

> ***That's not a small thing. That's the beginning of a relationship.***

Learning to Notice

The skill underneath this is noticing, developing the habit of paying attention to the small signals that routine transactions put in front of you constantly.

Some signals are in the transaction itself. A check that's larger than usual. A new address on a check order. A payment to an account you haven't seen before. A cash withdrawal that's out of character for this member. These details are there every day, in every transaction. Most of the time they pass without comment.

Some signals are in what the member says. The comment about a new job dropped while waiting for a receipt. The mention of a grandchild while asking about a wire transfer. The sigh that accompanies a question about an overdraft fee. The slightly distracted energy of someone whose mind is elsewhere.

And some signals are in what the member doesn't say, the question that seems to be hovering just behind the stated request, the hesitation that suggests something more complex is going on, the look of someone who came in for a transaction but might actually need a conversation.

You don't act on every signal. That would feel intrusive. But you notice them, and when one feels worth following, you follow it.

"New address on these checks, are you moving?"

"That's a big deposit, anything exciting behind it?"

"You look like you've got something on your mind. Everything okay?"

These questions are low-pressure. They give the member an easy out if they don't want to talk. But they signal something important: that you're paying attention to them as a person, not just processing their request as a task. And for members who are navigating something, who came in partly to handle a transaction and partly because something is happening in their financial life, that signal is often exactly what they needed to open up.

The Weight of Being Remembered

There's a specific kind of trust that builds when a member realizes you remember something they told you.

It doesn't take much. A member mentioned last month that she was thinking about buying a house. Today she's in to make a regular deposit. As she's about to leave, you ask: "Whatever happened with the house search?"

She stops. Looks slightly surprised. And then, almost always, she smiles.

Because being remembered means something. In most commercial interactions, you are your account number. You are your transaction history. You are not a person with a story that carries from one visit to the next. When a banker breaks that pattern, when they actually remember what you said, and ask about it, and seem genuinely interested in the update, it stands out in a way that's hard to articulate but easy to feel.

"How did the move go?"

"Is your daughter settling in at college?"

"Did you end up getting that truck?"

These questions take five seconds. They cost nothing. And they do more to build a lasting relationship than almost any product conversation could.

The practical challenge is remembering. Bankers see a lot of members, and members don't always come in on a predictable schedule. The solution isn't a perfect memory, it's a system. A note in the account. A quick detail written somewhere accessible. Something that lets you pick up the thread when the member walks back in two weeks or two months later.

The members who feel remembered become the members who come back. And the members who come back are the ones who eventually ask for you by name.

The Compound Effect

No single moment builds a relationship. What builds a relationship is the accumulation of moments, each one small, each one unremarkable on its own, together creating something durable.

Think about how this works over time.

A member comes in for the first time to open an account. You ask a question or two beyond the application. Nothing dramatic, just genuine interest. She leaves having been helped efficiently and treated like a person. A small positive impression.

She comes back a few weeks later for something routine. You recognize her. Maybe remember her name, or something she mentioned. Another small deposit into the relationship.

A few months pass. She comes in with a question about her account. You help her, then ask how things are going more broadly. She mentions she's been thinking about buying a car. You spend five minutes talking through it, not selling, just helping her think. She leaves feeling like she got something useful.

Six months after that, she's back. Before the banker can say anything, she asks: "Is the same person who helped me before here today?"

That's the compound effect. Nothing dramatic happened at any single point. But the accumulation of small, genuine interactions built something real. She's not a customer who uses this branch. She's a member who has a banker.

What the Transaction Is Really For

Here's a reframe worth sitting with.

The transaction is not the point. ***The transaction is the occasion.***

Every time a member walks in to deposit a check or ask about a fee or replace a card, they are presenting you with an occasion, a legitimate reason to interact with a person you might not otherwise have access to. The transaction is handled. That's the baseline. What happens in and around the transaction is the opportunity.

And the opportunity is almost always the same: learn something. Connect for a moment. Plant the seed of a relationship. Make this person feel, even slightly, like they matter to someone at this institution.

Some days the lobby is too busy and the pace is too fast and the most you can do is handle the transaction efficiently and warmly and that's enough. But on the days when there's a breath, when the interaction has even thirty extra seconds, that's when the habit of noticing and asking makes its difference.

Not every transaction becomes a conversation. Not every conversation becomes a relationship. But every relationship began somewhere. And more often than not, it began in exactly this way: a routine moment, a small question, a member who felt seen.

The Job, Seen Differently

If you approach your work as a series of transactions to be completed, the job will feel repetitive. The lobby fills, empties, fills again. The same requests cycle through. Nothing accumulates.

But if you approach each transaction as an occasion, as a brief window into someone's financial life, and a chance to be someone they remember, something shifts. The work becomes more interesting. Individual members become people you know, not just accounts you've served. And over time, the branch you work in starts to feel like a place where relationships actually exist.

That's what credit unions are supposed to be. That's the original promise, not just a place to bank, but a place where members belong and someone is looking out for them.

Turning that promise into a daily reality doesn't require a new program or a different product lineup. It requires the decision, made again and again in the small moments, to see the person behind the transaction.

And to ask one more question before they go.

In the next chapter, we'll look at one of the most valuable things a banker can offer, something products can't provide and the internet can't replace: helping members think clearly when a decision actually matters.

CHAPTER 8

Helping Members think Clearly

Here's something worth considering the next time a member sits down across from you with a financial question.

They didn't come to you because they couldn't find a loan online. They didn't come because rates are hard to research or because applications are difficult to fill out. All of that is available in minutes, from anywhere, at any hour.

They came because they're not sure what to do.

That distinction matters more than it might seem. A member who knows exactly what they want and just needs someone to process it is a transaction. A member who has a decision to make and isn't sure how to think about it, that's a person who needs a banker. Not the kind who processes applications. The kind who helps people think.

That kind of help is genuinely rare. It can't be automated. It can't be replicated by a comparison website or a chatbot or an online calculator. It requires someone with experience, judgment, and the willingness to slow down and actually engage with another person's specific situation.

That person is you. And when you show up that way, as a thinking partner rather than a transaction processor, what members feel is something they may not be able to name but will absolutely remember.

> *They feel clarity. And clarity, in financial decisions, is one of the most valuable things one person can offer another.*

What a Thinking Partner Actually Does

The phrase thinking partner is worth unpacking, because it's not the same as advisor, and it's not the same as expert.

An expert tells you what to do. An advisor recommends a course of action based on your situation. A thinking partner does something subtler and often more useful: they help you understand your own situation well enough to arrive at the right decision yourself.

This matters because most people, when they make an important financial decision, don't just want to be told what to do. They want to understand it. They want to feel like the decision came from their own thinking, shaped by good information and a clear view of the trade-offs. They want to walk out feeling confident, not because someone reassured them, but because they actually understood what they were deciding.

The thinking partner's job is to create that understanding.

It looks like slowing the conversation down when someone is moving too fast. Like asking a question that surfaces something the member hadn't considered. Like laying out options in plain language so the trade-offs become visible. Like pointing out the thing they might regret not knowing, even when they didn't ask.

It does not look like steering them toward a particular product. It does not look like enthusiastic agreement with whatever they're already leaning toward. It does not look like filling silence with information when what's needed is a question.

When you get this right, the member doesn't leave thinking "the banker told me to do this." They leave thinking "I made a good decision." And they associate that feeling with you.

The Questions That Create Clarity

Clarity almost always begins with questions, not because questions are a technique, but because most people haven't fully organized their thinking before they sit down. They know they have a decision to make. They have some facts, some instincts, some vague concerns. But they haven't worked through it systematically. They haven't named what they're optimizing for, or what they're most worried about, or what success actually looks like.

Good questions do that work. They create structure in a conversation that would otherwise meander toward the nearest available product.

If a member is thinking about buying a car, the questions aren't about the car. They're about the decision.

What made you start looking now?

How long do you expect to keep it?

What's the payment range that would let you sleep at night?

Is reliability the main thing, or is there something else driving this?

These questions help the member discover what they actually value, which is almost always more nuanced than what they said when they first sat down. And once that's visible, the right recommendation becomes obvious. Not because you figured it out for them. Because you asked them the right questions and let them figure it out themselves.

That's not a small skill. It's the central skill of this kind of banking. And it takes practice to develop the instinct for which question to ask next.

Explaining Without Overwhelming

One of the quietest ways bankers lose members is by explaining things in language the member doesn't actually understand.

Financial terminology is second nature to anyone who works in banking. APR, amortization, debt-to-income ratio, equity, liquidity, these are the vocabulary of the job. They're precise and efficient. Among colleagues, they're essential.

In a member conversation, they're often a barrier.

The member nods. They don't want to seem uninformed. They may have encountered these terms before and have a general sense of them. But when you ask them to actually make a decision based on their understanding of amortization, the foundation isn't there. They're making choices on top of a concept they haven't fully grasped.

Great bankers translate. They take the precise language of finance and render it in terms that are genuinely accessible.

> **Not this:** *This is a front-loaded amortization structure, which means your early payments are predominantly interest.*
>
> **But this:** *For the first few years, most of your payment goes toward interest rather than the balance. That changes over time, but early on, you're not paying down the principal as fast as it might feel like you are.*

Same information. Entirely different experience of receiving it.

When a member truly understands what's happening with their money, when the concept clicks rather than just passing through, something visible happens. Their posture changes slightly. They ask better questions. They engage with the decision rather than just accepting it. They feel like a participant rather than a passenger.

And they associate that clarity with the person who created it.

Walking Through the Trade-offs

One of the most useful things a banker can do, and one of the least commonly done, is lay out the options side by side and let the member see the trade-offs clearly.

Most of the time, members arrive with a preference already forming. They've been thinking about this. They have a direction. And most of the time, bankers respond to that preference directly, either affirming it and moving forward, or redirecting toward something else.

What's rarely done is stepping back and saying: let me show you both paths, and then you can tell me which one fits your situation better.

This is disarming in the best possible way. The member expected to be guided toward a product. Instead they're being invited to make an informed choice. That shift, from being sold to to being helped to decide, changes how they experience the entire conversation.

A member is weighing whether to use savings for a home repair or take out a small loan.

> *If you use your savings, you avoid the interest entirely and the repair is paid for immediately. The trade-off is that your cushion gets smaller, and if something else comes up before you rebuild it, you'd have less flexibility.*

> *If you finance it, your savings stay intact and you keep that cushion. The trade-off is the interest cost over the loan term, and a monthly payment for however long the loan runs.*

> *Neither is wrong. It depends on how you feel about your current savings level and how risk-averse you want to be with your cushion right now.*

Now the member has what they need to actually decide. They understand both paths. They can weigh them against their own priorities, their own comfort level, their own sense of what the right answer is for their life.

The banker didn't tell them what to do. The banker made it possible for them to know.

When the Best Advice Is "Not Yet"

This is the moment that separates bankers who are genuinely helpful from bankers who are professionally helpful.

Professionally helpful means doing what the member asked, completing the transaction, moving the interaction to a close. It's not wrong. It's just incomplete.

Genuinely helpful sometimes means saying something the member didn't come in to hear.

> *Before we go further, I want to make sure this payment fits comfortably into everything else you have going on.*
>
> *I want to show you what this looks like in the context of your full picture, because I think it might change how you're thinking about it.*
>
> *I'm a little concerned about the payment on this one. Can we look at it together?*

These moments require something. They require the banker to prioritize the member's financial well-being over the transaction at hand. To be willing to create a slight awkwardness, to slow something down that the member was ready to move forward on, because the numbers suggest they should pause.

Not every member will want to hear it. Some will push back. Some will say they've thought it through and they're ready to proceed. And that's their right, you help people make informed decisions, you don't make decisions for them.

But many members, when a banker gently raises a concern, will exhale. Because the concern was already there, somewhere. They were hoping someone would notice it. And when you notice it and name it, you become something more than a banker. You become someone they can trust to tell them the truth.

Those moments are the ones members remember for years.

Confidence Is the Real Product

It's worth saying plainly: the goal of all of this is not a product. The product is the mechanism. The goal is confidence.

A member who leaves a conversation feeling genuinely confident in their financial decision, who understands what they decided and why, who feels good about it, who doesn't spend the next week second-guessing themselves, has been well served. Regardless of which specific product they chose, or whether they chose a product at all.

Confidence like that comes from clarity. And clarity comes from the kind of conversation described in this chapter: curious, unhurried, honest about trade-offs, willing to slow down when something needs to be thought through more carefully.

When members experience that consistently, something changes in how they think about their financial life. They start making better decisions. They feel more capable of navigating their own finances. And they associate that capability, that growing sense of competence and confidence, with the banker who helped create it.

That's the long-term value of this work. Not the products sold. The people helped.

In the next chapter, we'll look at the conversations that test a banker's character most directly, the ones that happen when a member is struggling, and how the way you handle those moments shapes everything that follows.

CHAPTER 9

When Members Are Struggling

There is a version of this job that's easy to love.

A member comes in excited about buying their first home. A young couple sits down to open a joint account. Someone gets approved for a loan they've been working toward for months. These conversations have energy. They're easy to be present in. They feel like exactly what banking is supposed to be.

And then there are the other conversations.

A member whose card was declined at the grocery store and is trying to hold it together. Someone whose account has been overdrawn for the third time this month and who can feel the clerk's eyes on them when they explain why they're there. A member who has been managing a growing credit card balance in silence, trying not to think about it, and who has finally come in because ignoring it stopped working.

These conversations are harder. They carry a different weight. And for many bankers, especially early in a career, they're the ones that feel most uncertain. The training doesn't quite cover them. The scripts don't fit. There's no clear protocol for how to be genuinely useful to someone who is embarrassed and stressed and trying very hard not to show it.

But here's what's also true: these are some of the most important conversations you will ever have as a banker. Because how you handle a member in a difficult moment, what you say, how you listen, what you choose not to say, shapes the relationship more powerfully than almost anything else.

> ***Trust built in easy moments is ordinary. Trust built in hard ones is the kind that lasts.***

What the Member Is Carrying

Before thinking about what to say or do, it helps to understand what the member is actually experiencing when they walk through the door.

Financial stress is not like other kinds of stress. It's layered in a way that makes it particularly hard to talk about.

> **The practical layer:** *The actual problem. The overdraft. The declined card. The payment that didn't go through. Concrete, addressable, solvable. This is the part that prompted the visit.*

> **The emotional layer:** *Embarrassment. The sense that managing money is something adults are supposed to handle, and that struggling with it means something unflattering about you. Shame, especially if this isn't the first time.*

> **The fear underneath:** *Not necessarily about the immediate problem, but about what it might represent. Whether things are going in the wrong direction. Whether it's going to get worse before it gets better.*

Most members carrying all of this will not name it. They'll state the practical problem briefly, answer the questions they're asked, and try to get through the interaction as quickly as possible. Not because they don't need help, but because being seen clearly in this moment feels risky. They're not sure whether the person across the desk is safe.

Your first job, before any solution, before any explanation, before anything practical, is to make them feel that you are.

Starting With Empathy

Empathy in this context doesn't mean an elaborate emotional response. It means something simpler: a tone and a posture that tells the member they are not being judged.

A calm voice. Unhurried. Not clipped or professionally distant, but warm. The sense that you have time for this, even if the lobby is busy.

Eye contact that's steady without being intense. The physical signal that you're present with them, not already thinking about the next interaction.

And words that acknowledge the situation without dramatizing it.

Let's take a look together and figure out what's going on.

These things happen, let's see what we can do.

I'm glad you came in.

That last one is worth sitting with. "I'm glad you came in." Three words that do something significant: they reframe the act of coming to the branch not as an admission of failure but as a reasonable and even good thing to do. The member who has been dreading this conversation for two days needs to hear that it was the right call to show up.

What you're doing in these opening moments is not solving the problem. You're creating the conditions under which the problem can actually be talked about. That's a different task, and it has to come first.

Finding the Real Situation

Once the immediate pressure has eased, once the member feels less like they're sitting across from a judge and more like they're sitting across from someone who wants to help, a gentle question can open up the fuller picture.

Do you mind if I ask what's been going on more broadly?

Is this part of a bigger situation, or more of a one-time thing?

How long has this been going on?

These questions aren't intrusive when the tone has been established correctly. They're an invitation. And the member will decide how much to share.

Some will keep it brief. "Just a rough month." That's fine. You work with what you have.

But many will say more than you expected. A job that ended suddenly. A medical bill that arrived at the worst possible time. A divorce that upended everything financially. A period of things going sideways all at once that hasn't fully resolved yet.

When members share this, when they trust you with the real situation rather than just the surface problem, something has happened in the room. The relationship has moved. You're not just a banker processing a problem anymore. You're a person who knows something true about another person's life. And that changes what you're able to offer.

Because now you can help with the actual situation, not just the presenting symptom.

Helping Without Judgment

The role here is not to assess how the member got into this situation, and it is absolutely not to express any opinion about it. Financial struggles happen to people who are careful with money and people who aren't, to people who planned well and people who didn't, to people who had bad luck and people who made poor choices, and often to people experiencing some combination of all of the above.

None of that is your concern right now. Your concern is what comes next.

Help might look like practical solutions: reorganizing accounts so payments land more predictably, setting up balance alerts before problems happen rather than after, exploring whether a consolidation option could simplify the picture. These are real tools and they make real differences.

But sometimes the most useful thing isn't a product or a feature. It's a realistic, honest look at what's possible from here.

> *Here's what I think we can do in the short term. Here's what I'd suggest thinking about over the next few months. Here's what would help prevent this from happening again.*

A road forward, however modest, is often what the member most needs. Not a complete solution to everything, just enough clarity to see that the situation is manageable. That there's a next step. That they're not stuck.

That clarity is a form of relief. And relief, offered without judgment, builds trust faster than almost anything else in this work.

The Dignity of the Interaction

This deserves its own section because it's easy to underestimate and impossible to recover from when it goes wrong.

The member sitting across from you in a difficult moment is paying close attention, not to the solution, but to how they're being treated. They will remember very little of what you said six months from now. They will remember, with considerable precision, how the interaction felt.

> *Did you make them feel like a problem to be managed, or a person to be helped?*
>
> *Did your tone suggest impatience, or patience?*

Did anything in the conversation suggest that you found their situation surprising, or less than you'd expect from a responsible adult?

These signals are subtle. Members often can't name them directly. But they feel them. And the member who leaves a difficult conversation feeling respected, genuinely respected, not just professionally handled, is the member who comes back. Not just for the next transaction, but for guidance. For advice. For the kind of ongoing relationship that this book is about.

The member who leaves feeling diminished, even slightly, may not come back at all. Not because they found a better product somewhere else, but because they associate this place with how they felt in a vulnerable moment. And that association is hard to undo.

Dignity costs nothing to give. It requires only attention and intention. And it may be the most important thing you offer in these conversations.

What Gets Built Here

There's a common assumption in banking that relationships are built in the good moments, when someone is approved for a loan, when a financial goal is reached, when a member comes in excited about something happening in their life.

Those moments matter. But they're not where the deepest trust forms.

> ***The deepest trust forms when someone is struggling and the person across the desk doesn't flinch.***

When they're embarrassed and you treat them with complete normalcy. When they're worried and you help them see a path forward.

When they came in braced for judgment and left feeling, unexpectedly, like someone was genuinely on their side.

Members who experience that don't forget it. It becomes part of how they think about the credit union, and about you specifically. They recommend you to friends not because of a product feature but because of a feeling: when I was going through something, that person actually helped.

That's the kind of reputation that doesn't come from a marketing campaign. It comes from one hard conversation handled well. And then another. And then another.

The members who come back after a difficult moment are often the most loyal members you'll ever have. Because they know something about you that the ones who only came in on easy days don't.

They know that you show up when it matters.

In the next chapter, we'll shift to Part III, looking at the habits and reputation that, built over time, turn a good banker into the banker members seek out by name.

PART III

BECOMING THE BANKER MEMBERS ASK FOR

CHAPTER 10

The Banker Who Wins the Room

Every branch has one.

You probably already know who it is at yours, or you've worked somewhere that had one and you knew it then too. They're not necessarily the most senior person. They're not always the loudest or the most outwardly confident. But when they walk through the door, something shifts. Members who are waiting look up. People who have a choice about who to sit with tend to end up at their desk.

Other bankers notice it. They describe it the way people describe things they can't quite explain. "People just trust her." Or: "He's great with members." Or: "I don't know how she does it, they all ask for her."

The assumption is usually that it's personality. Some people are just naturally good with other people, and this person happens to be one of them. Maybe they're warmer, or more charismatic, or more extroverted, and that's just who they are.

But watch closely enough, and something else comes into focus.

The banker who wins the room isn't running on personality. They're running on habits, specific, learnable practices that shape how every member experiences every interaction. The warmth is real, but the warmth is not the whole explanation. What's underneath it is a set of decisions made consistently, over time, that add up to something members can feel even when they can't articulate it.

Habits can be built. The path from average to memorable isn't reserved for a particular kind of person.

Here's what those habits are.

HABIT 1

They Slow Down

Branch environments have a natural pace, and that pace is fast. Transactions stacking. Members waiting. The lobby a moving system of needs and requests and completions. There's always implicit pressure to move to the next thing.

The banker who wins the room has made a quiet decision about this pressure. They don't ignore it, they're not oblivious to the lobby, but they don't let it dictate every interaction either. They've learned that even thirty seconds of genuine unhurriedness changes the experience of the whole conversation.

It looks like pausing before reaching for the keyboard. Like asking a question before starting the transaction. Like finishing what the member is saying before responding. Like not signaling, through any small movement or expression, that you're already thinking about who's next.

What brings you in today?

That question, actually asked, actually heard, instead of the quick assumption that you already know what's needed. The pause costs almost nothing. What it creates is significant: the sense that this interaction, however brief, belongs to the member.

Relationships don't form at full speed. They need even a little space. The banker who creates that space, consistently, is the one people remember.

HABIT 2

They Make People Feel Safe

Money is one of the few topics that carries genuine social risk in a conversation. People worry about revealing ignorance. They worry about being judged for their choices. They worry that the banker across from them is already forming an opinion about their situation, their balance, their credit, their financial literacy.

This worry is often invisible. Members don't announce it. But it shapes how they behave: how much they share, how directly they ask their actual questions, whether they engage or simply try to get through the interaction as efficiently as possible.

The banker who wins the room dissolves this worry without drawing attention to it. They do it through consistency of tone, never reacting to a balance, a question, or a situation with anything that could be read as surprise or judgment. They do it through language that treats every question as reasonable and every situation as normal. They do it through patience, the willingness to explain something twice, or three times, without any trace of impatience.

Members sense this within the first minute. And once they feel it, they open up. They ask the questions they actually have. They share the situation they've been carrying. They stop managing the conversation and start having it.

That's when banking becomes useful in the fullest sense.

HABIT 3

They Listen More Than They Talk

There's a persistent belief in professional settings that expertise expresses itself through speaking. That knowing a lot means saying a lot. That demonstrating value means presenting, explaining, informing.

The banker who wins the room has discovered that this belief is mostly wrong, or at least, profoundly incomplete.

> ***Listening builds trust faster than talking.***

It demonstrates a different and deeper kind of expertise: the ability to understand a specific person's specific situation rather than deploying general knowledge in the general direction of whoever is sitting across the desk.

The mechanics of good listening are learnable. Full eye contact, not aggressive, just genuinely engaged. A nod that shows processing, not just waiting. A follow-up question that proves the previous answer was actually heard. Silence used as a tool, the deliberate choice not to fill every pause, allowing the member to finish a thought rather than being interrupted by the next question.

What this produces, in the member, is the experience of being genuinely heard. And genuine hearing is rarer than it should be, rare enough that when it happens, people notice it and feel something that might be described as relief. The relief of not having to fight to be understood.

The banker who wins the room doesn't win it by talking. They win it by listening in a way that makes members feel the conversation was actually about them.

HABIT 4

They Make the Complex Feel Simple

Financial concepts have a tendency to accumulate jargon. The people who work in financial services use this language constantly and have long since stopped noticing how opaque it is to people on the outside.

APR. Amortization. Origination fee. Debt-to-income ratio. Equity. These terms have precise meanings that matter. But deployed without translation in a member conversation, they create a subtle problem: the member nods along, not fully understanding, and makes decisions on top of that incomplete foundation.

The banker who wins the room translates. Not because they think members are incapable, but because they understand that clarity is a service, and that their job is not to display how much they know but to help the member understand their own situation.

> **Not:** *This loan has a front-loaded amortization schedule.*
> **But:** *In the early years, most of your payment goes toward interest rather than the balance. That shifts over time, but it's worth knowing upfront.*

The information is identical. The second version is simply accessible. And accessible information produces something the first version rarely does: a member who understands what they're agreeing to, feels confident about it, and associates that confidence with the person who helped create it.

HABIT 5
They Show Up the Same Way Every Time

Some bankers have great conversations when a member comes in for a significant loan. They slow down, ask good questions, take their time. The interaction feels important and they treat it that way.

The same bankers, when a member comes in to replace a lost card or ask a simple question, click into a different mode. Efficient. Transactional. Professional but not particularly present.

The banker who wins the room doesn't have two modes. They bring the same quality of attention to a debit card replacement that they bring to a mortgage application. Not the same amount of time, obviously, different transactions take different amounts of time, but the same quality of presence.

The simple deposit gets a question. The routine account change gets a moment of real engagement. The member who comes in for something small feels, even in that brief interaction, like someone paid attention to them.

Members don't segment their experience of you the way a transaction log does. They develop a general impression built from the accumulation of every interaction, small and large. The banker who wins the room is consistent across all of them.

That consistency is what trust is actually made of.

HABIT 6
They Follow Up

This is the rarest habit on the list. And because it's rare, it stands out more than almost anything else a banker can do.

Following up means, after a conversation about something that matters to a member, taking the initiative to check in. Not waiting for the member to come back with an update. Reaching out first.

> *Just wanted to check in, how is everything going with the new car?*
>
> *I've been thinking about what we talked about. How is the savings plan coming along?*
>
> *I wanted to follow up and see how things are going. Is there anything else I can help with?*

These messages don't need to be elaborate. A sentence or two is enough. What they communicate is something no product feature can communicate: you were still on my mind after you left. That the banker's interest in the member's situation didn't end when the transaction closed.

Most members have never experienced this from a financial institution. When it happens, it registers as remarkable. Not because it required a lot of effort, it didn't, but because it represents something genuinely uncommon: a banker who cares about the outcome, not just the interaction.

What These Habits Add Up To

Taken individually, each of these habits is modest. Slowing down. Making people feel safe. Listening well. Explaining clearly. Showing up consistently. Following up.

None of them are dramatic. None require a particular personality type. None are beyond reach for anyone willing to practice them deliberately.

But taken together, over time, applied consistently across hundreds and then thousands of interactions, they produce something that can't be manufactured or shortcutted: a reputation. The specific reputation of being the banker people seek out. The one members walk in asking for. The one colleagues point new members toward. The one who, without having done anything flashy or unconventional, has simply made every person feel like they mattered.

That's what winning the room actually means.

Not performance. Not charm. Not a particular kind of personality.

Just the decision, made again and again, to show up fully for whoever is sitting across from you, and the habits that make that possible.

In the next chapter, we'll look at what happens when these habits have been practiced long enough that something changes permanently, when you stop being a banker members visit and become the banker members come back to.

CHAPTER 11

Becoming Their Banker

There's a moment that happens quietly, without announcement, and easy to miss if you're not paying attention.

A member walks into the branch. They don't approach the first available desk. They scan the room. They're looking for someone specific. And when they find you, something in their posture settles.

I was hoping you'd be here.

Or they call ahead. Or they schedule time rather than just walking in. Or they stop by not because they have a transaction to complete but because they have a question they've been holding onto, waiting for the right moment to ask.

This is not a small thing. In a world where financial products are increasingly available everywhere, online, in apps, through any number of institutions, the decision to seek out a specific person represents something that can't be replicated by a website or automated by an algorithm. It represents trust. Not institutional trust, but personal trust. The kind where the individual matters.

That moment, when a member walks in looking for you, is what this chapter is about. How it happens. What it means. And what it asks of you once it does.

The Difference Between a Banker and Their Banker

It's worth being precise about what changes when this shift occurs, because the difference is more significant than it might appear.

Before the shift, a member's relationship with the credit union is primarily institutional. They have an account. They complete transactions. The experience is professional and adequate. Which banker helps them on any given day doesn't much matter, any competent person will do.

After the shift, something personal has been layered on top of the institutional. The member now has a person they associate with their financial life. Someone whose opinion they value. Someone they bring their uncertainty to before they act, not after. Someone who, when a financial decision comes up, they think of almost automatically.

The difference in behavior is visible. Before: the member completes transactions and leaves. After: the member lingers, asks questions that weren't part of the stated purpose of the visit, mentions things happening in their life, checks in about things you discussed last time.

And for the banker, the difference in how the work feels is hard to overstate. The job becomes something other than a series of transactions. It becomes a set of relationships, some newer, some years old, that give the work meaning and make the days genuinely interesting.

How It Starts

The shift from banker to their banker doesn't happen in a single conversation. It can't be manufactured or forced. It grows from the accumulation of small moments, most of them unremarkable at the time.

A question asked during a routine transaction that made the member feel noticed. An explanation offered that made something complicated suddenly clear. A follow-up a few weeks later that showed the previous conversation hadn't been forgotten. A moment when a concern was raised gently, "I want to make sure this fits your situation before we move forward", that the member interpreted correctly as someone looking out for them.

None of these are dramatic. Each one, alone, is ordinary. But members are paying attention, not consciously cataloging every interaction but forming an impression over time. And the impression that forms, when a banker consistently shows up with curiosity and care and honesty, is:

> ***This person is actually on my side.***

That impression is the foundation. Everything else is built on it.

The First Signs

The early signals that a relationship is forming are subtle, and worth recognizing when they appear.

> **1. Questions beyond the transaction,** *They came in to deposit a check. The transaction is done. But then: "Can I ask you something?" These questions represent a decision to bring you into something they're thinking about.*

> **2. Unprompted disclosure,** *A member who volunteers context that wasn't asked for, who shares details about their life or situation, is signaling comfort. They've decided you're someone it's safe to be honest with.*

> **3. The deliberate return,** *When a member who could go online, call the main number, or use any branch consistently chooses to come to you specifically, that choice is meaningful.*

When these signals appear, the appropriate response is not to escalate or capitalize but to receive them carefully. To answer the question with the same honesty and care that earned the question in the first place. To be worthy of what's being offered.

Helping Before They Ask

One of the characteristics that distinguishes the most trusted bankers is a kind of proactive attentiveness, the habit of noticing things and saying something about them, even when the member hasn't asked.

This is different from selling. Selling is noticing an opportunity and presenting a product. Proactive attentiveness is noticing something about a member's situation and raising it in service of their interests, whether or not it leads to a transaction.

A member mentions casually that their daughter just started college. A trusted banker might say: "How are you thinking about the financial side of that?", not because there's a product to sell, but because that's a real question with real implications.

A member deposits a check from the sale of their home. A trusted banker might ask: "Big transition, what are you thinking about doing next?", not to pitch investment products, but because a major financial event is a natural moment to help someone think clearly.

These moments communicate something important about the nature of the relationship. The banker's attention doesn't turn off when the transaction closes. Members notice this. It confirms what they've been gradually coming to believe: that this person actually thinks about them.

The Responsibility That Comes With Trust

When a member begins relying on you for guidance, something shifts in the nature of the role. The obligation is no longer just to complete transactions competently. It's to be genuinely trustworthy, to give advice that serves the member's actual interests, even when that's inconvenient, even when it doesn't produce a product.

This means being willing to say things that are easier not to say.

> *I'm not sure this is the right move right now.*
>
> *Before you go forward, there's something I want you to consider.*
>
> *Honestly, I think waiting six months would put you in a better position.*

These moments require the willingness to prioritize the member's financial well-being over the transaction at hand. Most members will never directly thank you for this kind of honesty. But they feel it. And it does more to deepen the relationship than almost anything else you can offer.

There's also a quieter dimension to this responsibility: consistency. A member who has come to think of you as their banker has extended a kind of ongoing trust. That trust is renewed or eroded with every interaction.

Being someone's banker isn't a destination. It's a practice. Something that has to be tended.

What a Decades-Long Relationship Looks Like

Some banking relationships span the arc of a financial life, and it's worth pausing on what that actually means.

A member opens her first checking account at 22. A young banker asks a few genuine questions and takes the time to explain how overdraft protection works in plain terms. She leaves feeling like someone at the credit union actually paid attention.

- She comes back. She refers a roommate.
- A few years later: a first car loan. The banker helps her think through what she can comfortably afford.
- A few years after that: a mortgage conversation.
- Then a refinance. Then a question about savings strategies when a baby arrives.
- Then college funds. Then, eventually, conversations about retirement.

At each stage, the banker has been part of how she navigated an important financial decision. Not by telling her what to do, but by helping her think clearly, offering honest perspective, and occasionally saying the thing she needed to hear rather than the thing that was easiest to say.

That relationship represents something genuinely valuable, not just in commercial terms, though it certainly is that. It represents years of trust, maintained through consistency and honesty and care. And for the banker, it represents what the job can be at its best: not a series of transactions, but a presence in another person's financial life that made a real difference over time.

The Work, at Its Best

Banking is often described from the outside as a business of products and numbers. And products and numbers matter, they're the mechanism through which financial goals are reached and financial problems are solved.

But the bankers who find the work genuinely meaningful tend to describe something different as the source of that meaning. Not the rate they offered. Not the loan they closed. The relationship. The member who came back after a hard year and said things are finally starting to turn around. The young couple who got the house. The member who was in real trouble and found a path forward. The person who came in for a routine transaction and left understanding their finances a little better than when they arrived.

These are the things that stay. And they're available, not to some special category of banker, not to those with a particular gift or personality, but to anyone willing to practice the discipline described in this book.

Becoming their banker isn't about being exceptional.

It's about being consistent. Honest. Curious. Genuinely interested in the person across the desk.

Do that, over time, with enough people, and the relationships form on their own.

In the next chapter, we'll look at what happens when that kind of relationship extends beyond the branch, when your reputation for advice begins to travel, and members start coming to you because of what someone else told them.

CHAPTER 12

Building a Reputation for Advice

Think about the professionals in your life you genuinely trust.

Not the ones you use because they're convenient, or because the reviews are solid, or because someone has to do the job and they showed up. The ones you actually trust. The mechanic you call before you take your car anywhere else. The doctor who actually listens. The accountant your family has used for twenty years. The real estate agent your neighbors recommended and who turned out to be exactly what was described.

What do these people have in common?

They're not necessarily the most credentialed in their field. They're not always the most experienced. What they share is something more specific: a reputation for giving honest, useful guidance that puts the other person's interests first. A reputation built not from marketing but from experience, from the accumulated impressions of people who sat across from them and came away feeling genuinely helped.

That's the kind of reputation this chapter is about. The kind that travels through communities through word of mouth, that precedes you into conversations with members you've never met, that takes years to build and, once built, changes the nature of your work entirely.

It's the most valuable professional asset a banker can develop. And it starts with a single conversation.

How Reputation Actually Forms

There's a common misconception about professional reputation: that it's something you build deliberately, through strategy and positioning and careful management of how you're perceived.

That's not how it works. Not really. Not the kind that matters.

The reputation that lasts forms the way trust forms, slowly, incrementally, from the accumulation of individual experiences that each leave a small impression. A member who felt helped. A conversation that went beyond the transaction. An explanation that actually made something clear. A moment when a banker raised a concern the member was grateful someone finally named.

Each of these experiences creates a small deposit. Most of them the banker never knows about, the member who goes home and tells their spouse what a good conversation they had, or mentions the credit union to a friend who's been unhappy with their bank, or brings their adult child in because they want them to meet the person who's been helping them.

Over time, these deposits accumulate into something that has a life of its own. People start arriving with a prior expectation, "I heard she's really helpful", which makes the relationship easier to establish. Your name starts appearing in conversations you weren't part of. Members you've never met tell you, when they sit down for the first time, that a friend sent them.

> ***That's a reputation. You didn't declare it. It formed from what you actually did, and how people actually felt, and what they said to other people afterward.***

Why Advice Travels

Of all the things a member might recommend about a financial institution, products are rarely the thing that actually spreads. Rates change. Features get matched. What people talk about, what they actually tell their friends, is an experience.

Specifically: the experience of being genuinely helped with a financial decision.

Financial decisions are stressful. Buying a home, choosing a car loan, figuring out debt, planning for something in the future, these decisions carry real weight, and most people navigate them without access to anyone who can help them think clearly. They research online, read articles that don't quite apply to their situation, ask friends who know as much as they do, and eventually make a decision they feel somewhere between uncertain and resigned about.

When a member finds someone who actually helps them, who slows down, asks the right questions, explains the trade-offs clearly, and offers honest perspective, it's a genuinely uncommon experience. Memorable not because it was elaborate, but because it was rare.

And rare positive experiences get talked about.

Not through formal reviews or testimonials, though those happen too. Through the organic, unremarkable conversations of daily life.

> *"You should talk to the person who helped us. She was really different."*

That's the sentence. Simple. Specific. And more convincing than anything a marketing department could produce, because it comes from someone with no reason to say it other than that it's true.

The Ripple Beyond the Branch

A reputation for advice doesn't stay contained within the member relationship that produced it. It travels, to spouses and partners who weren't present for the original conversation. To adult children who are now making their own financial decisions. To friends and neighbors and coworkers who happen to mention they're thinking about buying a house, or refinancing, or finally trying to get their savings organized.

Each of these referrals arrives with something that takes months to build from scratch: a prior sense of trust. The referred member walks in already expecting to be helped, already inclined to engage, already open to the kind of conversation that takes longer than a transaction but produces something real.

This is what makes reputation so compounding in its effect. Every member who has a genuinely good experience becomes a potential source of future relationships. And those relationships, because they begin from a position of established credibility, tend to develop more quickly and go deeper than ones that start cold.

The practical implication is worth naming directly: a banker who focuses on advice, who consistently prioritizes helping members over processing transactions, is not sacrificing productivity for principle. They're building a pipeline. Slowly, invisibly, member by member, creating a network of relationships that generates new opportunities without effort or strategy, simply because people tell other people about experiences that mattered.

The Ripple Inside the Institution

The reputation doesn't only travel outward into the community. It travels inward too, through the credit union itself.

Managers notice when members ask for a specific banker. They notice when someone who could have gone to any desk, or done the whole thing online, chose to come in and wait. They notice when members mention names in exit surveys, or say something at the front desk, or call to speak with someone specific.

Over time, a pattern becomes visible. This person produces not just transactions but relationships. Members who come back. Members who bring family. Members who were referred by members.

That pattern creates opportunities. Not necessarily through formal advancement, though often it contributes there too, but through the kind of internal credibility that comes from being known as someone who does the work well in a way that's hard to fake. Someone managers trust to handle difficult conversations. Someone newer colleagues watch and try to learn from. Someone the institution recognizes as genuinely valuable in ways that don't always show up cleanly on a scoreboard.

Reputation Is Earned, Not Claimed

This point is worth stating plainly, because it runs counter to how reputation is often discussed in professional contexts.

You cannot build a reputation for advice by saying you give great advice. You cannot establish trustworthiness through a personal brand or a LinkedIn description or a carefully curated set of testimonials. These things may have their uses, but they are not reputation in the sense meant here.

Reputation is what members decide about you based on their experience of you. It's formed in the moments after the conversation ends, in what the member says to their spouse on the way home, or to a friend who asks how it went, or to themselves when they're deciding whether to come back. You don't control those moments. You only influence them, through what you actually do in the conversation itself.

The question is simple, even if the practice of it takes years to develop:

> *Did they leave feeling genuinely helped?*

Not efficiently handled. Not professionally processed. Genuinely helped, in a way that made a real difference to a real decision in their real life.

When the answer to that question is consistently yes, the reputation forms on its own. And once formed, it does work on your behalf that no amount of deliberate reputation-building ever could.

What the Reputation Actually Says

When a member refers someone to you, they're making a claim about you. They're putting their own credibility on the line, saying, in effect: this person helped me, and I believe they'll help you too.

That's a meaningful act. People don't make it carelessly. They make it when the experience was significant enough to remember and specific enough to describe. When it wasn't just a pleasant interaction but something that actually made a difference.

The reputation that matters most is not "she's nice" or "they're professional" or "it's a good credit union." It's something more specific. Something that names what you actually do.

> *She helped me think through the decision before I made it.*

> *He told me something I needed to hear that I wouldn't have figured out on my own.*

> *She didn't just process my loan, she helped me understand what I was signing.*

These sentences are the reputation. They describe a banker who showed up as an advisor rather than a salesperson, who cared about the outcome rather than the transaction, who was genuinely useful in a moment that mattered.

Build enough of those sentences, said by enough people, in enough conversations you'll never know about, and the reputation is real.

In the next chapter, we'll look at what all of this means for a career, and why the approach described in this book produces better results over time than any alternative.

PART IV

THE CAREER AND IMPACT OF ADVICE-BASED BANKING

CHAPTER 13

The Career Advantage of Advice-Based Banking

Early in a banking career, success is measured in fairly legible terms.

Products opened. Loans approved. Accounts added. The branch scoreboard. The monthly numbers. These metrics are visible and immediate, they tell you, in concrete terms, how a particular week or month went. And they matter. Credit unions need strong performance. The numbers aren't arbitrary.

But there's a different question worth asking, one that doesn't appear on any report: what kind of banker are you becoming?

Because the habits you build early, how you approach member conversations, what you're optimizing for in each interaction, what you consider a successful outcome, compound over time. The banker who spends their first few years practicing curiosity, guidance, and honest advice is developing something that will serve them for the rest of their career. The banker who spends those same years optimizing purely for transaction counts is also developing something. Just something different.

This chapter is about the long arc. About what advice-based banking produces over time, not just for members, but for the person practicing it. About why the approach that seems slower in the short term tends to produce better outcomes by almost every measure in the long term. And about what a career built on trust looks like, from the inside.

The Short Game vs. the Long Game

There's a version of banking that optimizes for the immediate transaction. A member arrives, a product is identified, the application is processed, the number moves on the board. Clean, efficient, repeatable. And in any given week, this approach produces results that look solid.

The problem is what it doesn't produce: relationships. And relationships are where the compounding happens.

A member who trusts a banker doesn't just do one transaction and leave. They come back. They bring the next decision, the auto loan six months after the checking account, the mortgage conversation a few years after that, the question about savings when the second child arrives. Over a five or ten-year period, a single relationship with a member who genuinely trusts you can represent more value, in products, in referrals, in the new members they bring in, than dozens of transactional interactions with members who had no particular reason to return.

This is not a theory. It's arithmetic. A member who feels helped becomes a member who comes back. A member who comes back brings their financial life with them, incrementally, over time. And a member who comes back also talks, to their spouse, their adult children, their friends and colleagues who are in similar life stages and facing similar decisions.

> ***The short game produces numbers. The long game produces a practice.***

A growing, self-reinforcing network of relationships that generates opportunities without requiring constant effort to create them from scratch.

What Changes When Opportunities Come to You

There's a specific shift that happens for bankers who have been practicing advice-based banking long enough that their reputation has formed. It's worth describing directly, because it changes the texture of the work in ways that are hard to anticipate.

The shift is this: you stop chasing and start receiving.

In the early stages, every opportunity requires effort to create. A member comes in for one thing; you have to find the moment to ask about something else. You're looking for the opening, creating the context, working to extend the conversation beyond its stated purpose.

Over time, as trust builds and reputation travels, something different begins to happen. Members arrive already thinking about things they want to discuss. They've been holding questions, waiting for the next visit. They call ahead to schedule time rather than just walking in. They bring a spouse or a parent or a friend, specifically because they want that person to meet you. The opportunities don't need to be manufactured. They arrive.

This doesn't mean the work becomes passive, it never does. But it becomes more natural. The energy that was spent finding the opening gets redirected toward the conversation itself. And the conversations are richer, because members who arrive with trust already established are more open, more honest, more willing to share the full picture of their situation.

That's the career dividend of consistent advice-based banking. Not just more members, but better conversations. More meaningful work, more days that feel like the job was worth doing.

What It Looks Like Inside the Institution

The reputation doesn't only affect the member relationship. It affects how you're perceived inside the credit union itself, and over time that internal reputation shapes your career in ways that are worth understanding.

Managers notice patterns. When members ask for a specific banker by name, that gets noticed. When a difficult conversation gets handled well, when a member who came in frustrated leaves feeling supported, someone is usually aware of that. When a banker consistently produces not just transactions but returning members and referrals, the pattern becomes visible.

What this creates, over time, is a different kind of institutional standing. Not just a good performer, but a trusted one. Someone whose judgment managers rely on for the harder situations. Someone newer colleagues watch and informally learn from. Someone who gets asked to participate in training, or to handle the relationship with a particularly important member, or to take on a responsibility that requires not just technical competence but the kind of credibility that comes from being known as someone who does the work well.

This kind of standing doesn't come from chasing advancement. It comes from being genuinely good at the work in a way that's visible to the people around you. And because it's earned rather than claimed, it tends to be more durable than credentials or titles alone.

The Confidence That Comes From Clarity

There's a psychological dimension to this that's worth naming, because it affects how the work feels day to day.

Banking that's organized around product goals can be quietly stressful in a way that's easy to absorb as normal. The pressure to find the moment. The awareness of the scoreboard. The slight friction of conversations where your objective and the member's objective aren't entirely aligned. Over time, this low-grade pressure shapes the experience of the job in ways that are hard to articulate but easy to feel.

Advice-based banking creates a different experience. When your objective is genuinely to help the member make a good decision, when that's the actual goal, not a means to a product outcome, the conversation becomes simpler. You ask questions. You listen. You share what you know. You recommend what actually makes sense for this person. There's no performance in it. No gap between what you're trying to do and what you're presenting yourself as trying to do.

That alignment produces confidence. Not the performed confidence of someone managing a pitch, but the quieter confidence of someone who knows what they're there to do and is simply doing it. Members feel this. It's one of the reasons advice-based bankers tend to build trust more quickly, the absence of agenda is perceptible, even when members can't name what they're responding to.

And that confidence compounds with experience. The more conversations you've had, the more situations you've navigated, the more you've seen what helps and what doesn't, the more naturally and surely the guidance comes. The work gets better and it gets easier, at the same time, which is a combination that doesn't happen in many careers.

Skills That Transfer Everywhere

Something else is building throughout this process, largely invisibly: a set of skills that extend well beyond the specific context of branch banking.

> *The ability to ask a question that opens up a situation.*
>
> *The ability to listen and actually understand what someone needs, rather than what they said.*
>
> *The ability to explain something complex in language that's genuinely accessible.*
>
> *The ability to help a person think clearly about a decision they're emotionally close to.*
>
> *The ability to deliver an honest perspective the other person needs to hear, even when it's uncomfortable.*

These are not banking skills. They're human skills, the skills of effective communication, of genuine influence, of leadership in the fullest sense of the word. They happen to be practiced in the context of member conversations. But they transfer.

The banker who has spent years guiding members through financial decisions has been, in parallel, developing the capacity to guide people through any consequential decision. That capacity shows up in management, in mentoring, in any situation that requires earning trust, communicating clearly, and helping someone navigate something difficult.

This is one of the underappreciated dimensions of advice-based banking as a career foundation. The skills you're building are not narrow. They prepare you for almost anything that requires working effectively with people, which is most of what leadership at any level actually requires.

The Meaning Question

At some point in most careers, often around the five or ten year mark, sometimes earlier, sometimes later, people start asking a question that the early years of professional life tend to suppress: does this actually matter?

It's a fair question. And banking, practiced in a purely transactional way, doesn't always offer a compelling answer. The numbers move. The products get sold. The institution performs. But the individual's sense of connection to any larger purpose can be genuinely hard to locate.

Advice-based banking answers the question differently.

When you helped that 28-year-old understand what she could comfortably afford in a first home, and she bought it, and two years later she came in with a photo of the finished nursery, that mattered. When you told a member that the payment was going to be harder than he thought, and he came back six months later to say he'd waited and now he was in a much better position, that mattered. When a member who had been in real financial trouble found a path forward because someone took twenty minutes to look at the full picture with them instead of just processing the surface problem, that mattered.

> *These moments don't appear in monthly reports. They're not metrics. But they're the substance of a career that feels worthwhile.*

The work is the same. The products are the same. What changes is how you use the conversations, and what you're producing with them.

Here's what tends to happen, over the span of a career built around advice and guidance:

- Members trust you. Not just the ones you've worked with for years, but new members who arrive already expecting to be helped because someone they trust sent them.

- Your time fills with conversations rather than cold interactions. The work becomes more interesting because the conversations go deeper.

- Inside the institution, your standing grows in ways that produce real opportunity, not because you've marketed yourself, but because the evidence of how you work is visible to the people who matter.

- The work feels like it's worth doing. You can point to specific people whose financial lives are meaningfully better because of conversations you had with them.

That's the career advantage of advice-based banking. Not a faster path to a particular title. Not a shortcut to a scoreboard. Something less legible and more durable than either of those things.

A career built on something real.

In the next chapter, we'll look at the members on the other side of these conversations, what they carry away, what they remember, and why the banker who helped them stays with them long after the details of the transaction have faded.

CHAPTER 14

The Banker Members Remember

Try asking someone about their financial history sometime.

Not the details, not what rate they got, or which institution they used, or what the terms were on the loan they took out twelve years ago. Most people don't remember any of that. Ask instead about the experiences. About the moments in their financial life that actually stayed with them.

What you'll find, consistently, is that people remember very little about products and quite a lot about people.

They remember the banker who sat with them for an extra twenty minutes when they were trying to decide whether they could actually afford the house. They remember the person who explained something in a way that finally made sense, after months of feeling confused about it. They remember who was patient with them when they were embarrassed. Who told them the truth when they needed to hear it. Who called to check in after a difficult conversation, when they hadn't expected anyone to follow up.

> ***They don't remember the rate. They remember the person.***

This chapter is about that phenomenon, what creates it, why it matters, and what it means for how you do your job.

Why Experiences Outlast Information

There's a well-established pattern in how human memory works that's directly relevant here: emotional experiences are encoded more durably than factual information.

A number, a rate, a term, a balance, is just a number. The brain files it somewhere accessible for a while and eventually lets it go. But an experience that carried emotional weight, the anxiety of a first mortgage, the relief of finding a path through a difficult financial period, the quiet pride of getting something right, that gets stored differently. It gets attached to the context, to the physical setting, to the people who were present.

This is why financial decisions are so memorable even when the financial details aren't. The decision to buy the first home was terrifying and exciting and felt enormous. Twelve years later, the member doesn't know what rate they got. But they remember sitting across from a banker who helped them understand what they could comfortably afford, who made the calculation feel manageable, who said something that let them exhale.

They remember the feeling. And the feeling is attached to a person.

This isn't a soft observation about the power of kindness. It's a practical reality about how trust forms and what produces lasting loyalty. Members return to people who helped them feel capable and confident during important moments. Not because they evaluated the interaction and decided it was optimal. Because the experience was memorable, and memory drives behavior.

The Moments That Carry Weight

Not every banking interaction carries the same emotional weight, and it's worth understanding which ones do, because those are the conversations where what you do matters most.

The first mortgage is one. The anxiety of that decision is real and significant. Most people have no idea whether they're making the right choice, whether the numbers actually work the way they think they do, whether they're ready. A banker who helps them think through it clearly, who asks the right questions, explains the trade-offs honestly, and helps them arrive at a decision they actually understand, is present at a genuinely important moment in their life.

A serious financial difficulty is another. The member who came in embarrassed, carrying stress they'd been managing alone for months, and found someone who treated them with respect and helped them see a way forward, that experience is not forgotten. The emotional relief of being helped when things were hard is one of the most durable impressions a banker can make.

A first major independent financial decision. A conversation about retirement for the first time. A moment when a banker said something honest that the member needed to hear. Any interaction where someone felt genuinely supported rather than processed.

These are the moments that produce memories. And memories, in banking, produce loyalty.

The Influence You Don't See

Most of what a banker produces is invisible to them.

A member leaves a conversation feeling more confident about a decision they've been worried about for weeks. They go home and describe the conversation to their spouse in a way that brings their partner's anxiety down too. They move forward. The decision turns out well. Their financial situation improves. Years later, when someone they know mentions they're trying to figure out the same kind of thing, they say: "you should talk to the person who helped us."

The banker who had that original conversation will never know most of this happened. They won't know that the conversation rippled outward into a household, or that it contributed to a financial decision that went well, or that it produced a referral six years later that they have no way of tracing to its origin.

This invisibility is one of the stranger features of the work. The impact is real, and often significant, and almost entirely out of view.

What it means practically is that the quality of any given conversation matters more than it might appear in the moment. The interaction that feels routine to you, just another conversation on an ordinary Tuesday, may be anything but routine to the member sitting across from you. They may have been thinking about this for months. They may be telling their family about it tonight. The conversation you're having is, from their perspective, potentially one of the more significant financial interactions of their year.

> ***Holding that awareness, even lightly, changes how you show up.***

What Gets Passed Down

Financial decisions don't just affect the person making them. They ripple outward, into households, into families, across generations.

The member who felt helped and confident at a critical moment often becomes someone who passes that forward. Not just through referrals, though those happen. Through the way they talk about money with their children. Through the example they model of approaching financial decisions thoughtfully rather than anxiously. Through the story they tell about the time things were difficult, and what helped.

Banking sits, sometimes without fully recognizing it, at a point of genuine leverage in people's financial lives. A conversation that helps someone understand their options more clearly, or feel more capable of navigating their finances, can influence the financial habits and attitudes of everyone that person is close to.

This doesn't mean every interaction needs to carry the weight of that awareness. Most conversations are ordinary, and that's fine, most conversations should be efficient and warm and appropriate to whatever the member actually needs. But it does mean that the work is not trivial. The conversations that go well, that leave members feeling genuinely helped, have effects that extend beyond what's visible in the branch.

A Different Measure

In banking, success is usually measured in metrics that are easy to count. Products opened, loans approved, balances grown. These numbers matter, they're how institutions track performance and make decisions.

But they don't capture the full picture of what the work produces.

There's another way to measure a banking career, and it's not one that appears in any report. It's the answer to a different set of questions.

How many people left your desk understanding their finances better than when they arrived?

How many important decisions were made more clearly, more confidently, because of a conversation you had?

How many members came back, not because they needed a transaction, but because they wanted your perspective?

How many people, in the years after a conversation you barely remember, told someone else that a banker at the credit union actually helped them?

These outcomes don't show up on a scoreboard. But they are what a career in this work actually produces, when it's done well. They're the substance underneath the metrics. The thing the metrics are trying to approximate but never quite capture.

The Story Members Tell

Years from now, some of the members you help will tell a story about a financial moment that mattered. They won't tell it often, just occasionally, when it's relevant, when someone is going through something similar, when the memory surfaces.

The story won't be about the product. It won't start with the rate or the term or the account type. It will start with a person, and a conversation, and what that conversation made possible.

> *When we were trying to figure out whether we could actually afford a house, the banker we worked with sat down with us and really*

> *helped us think it through. She didn't just approve the loan, she helped us understand what we were getting into.*

> *When things were really difficult financially, I went in not knowing what to do. The banker I talked to actually listened. He didn't make me feel like an idiot. He helped me figure out next steps.*

> *I almost made a really bad financial decision. The banker told me something I didn't want to hear, but it was the right thing to say. I'm glad she said it.*

These are the stories. Not elaborate. Not dramatic. But specific and genuine, the kind of story people only tell about experiences that were real.

The banker in each one did something that turned out to matter more than they probably knew. They helped someone think clearly at a moment when clarity was hard to find. They treated a person with respect when that person needed it. They told the truth when it would have been easier to stay quiet.

That's the work, at its best.

And it's the work members remember.

In the final chapter, we'll bring it all back to the idea that started this book, the three words that, practiced consistently, make everything else in these pages possible.

CHAPTER 15

Advice Before Products

Three words.

That's what this book comes down to, in the end. Three words that are simple enough to say in a breath and take a career to fully practice.

> *Advice before products.*

Not because products don't matter, they do. They're the mechanism through which financial goals become possible, through which problems get solved, through which members move from where they are to where they want to be. Products matter enormously.

But they're the answer, not the starting point. And the difference between starting with the answer and starting with the question is the difference between a transaction and a relationship. Between a member who got what they asked for and a member who was actually helped. Between a banker who processed a request and a banker who changed how someone thought about a decision.

That difference accumulates. Across hundreds of conversations and dozens of members and years of consistent practice, it accumulates into something that no product catalog or interest rate can produce: trust. The deep, durable, personal kind. The kind that makes members walk past other desks to find you.

The Simplest Description of the Job

If you had to describe advice-based banking in the plainest possible terms, stripped of frameworks and models and all the vocabulary that accumulates around any professional practice, it would sound something like this:

Understand the person before recommending the solution.

That's it. In ten words. Before you reach for the product, understand who is sitting across from you and what they're actually trying to accomplish. Everything else in this book, the pyramid, the GUIDE model, the five conversations, the habits, the questions, all of it is in service of that single, simple practice.

It sounds obvious stated this plainly. And in a sense it is, it's the way good advisors in any field have always worked, in any context where trust matters more than throughput. But obvious doesn't mean easy, and simple doesn't mean automatic. The pull toward the product is real. The pace of the branch is real. The pressure of the scoreboard is real. Practicing this consistently, day after day, in every interaction including the ones that don't feel important, that takes intentionality. It takes the decision to keep orienting toward the person when the path of least resistance leads toward the product.

That decision, made repeatedly, is what the discipline looks like in practice.

The First Moment of Judgment

There's a framing that has appeared throughout this book and is worth returning to now, as we near the end.

> ***Retail bankers are the first stewards of judgment in the financial institution.***

Before the underwriting model evaluates the application. Before the credit policy determines what's permissible. Before any approval or denial is issued. There is a conversation. A member sits down and begins to share what they're thinking about doing financially. And in that conversation, a banker has the opportunity to shape what comes next, not by overriding any policy, but by helping the member understand their situation more clearly before anything is decided.

That's a form of influence that doesn't show up anywhere in the org chart. It's quiet and invisible and happens dozens of times a day in every branch. But it matters. The conversation that helps a member think clearly before they apply leads to better applications, better decisions, and outcomes that work. The conversation that rushes past understanding toward the product leads to something else, sometimes a mismatch, sometimes a decision the member later regrets, sometimes a relationship that never forms because the member sensed they were managed rather than helped.

The quality of that first conversation shapes everything downstream. Which is why it deserves the kind of attention this book has tried to give it.

What Members Are Actually Looking For

Members don't walk into a credit union expecting a perfect banker. They don't arrive with a checklist of qualities or a set of standards they're quietly evaluating you against.

What most of them are looking for is much simpler, and harder to find than it should be.

Someone who will listen to what they're actually saying rather than preparing a response while they're still talking. Someone who will explain something complicated in terms that are genuinely accessible, without making them feel like they should have already known it. Someone who will help them think through a decision rather than tell them what to do. Someone who, when they raise a concern about the member's situation, is clearly doing it because they care about the outcome.

That combination is not common. In most financial service interactions, members are processed efficiently and professionally, and that's it. The experience is fine. It's just not memorable. It doesn't produce trust. It doesn't produce loyalty. It doesn't produce the member who calls ahead to schedule time with a specific person because they have a question they've been holding onto.

When members find a banker who offers this kind of guidance, who actually listens, who explains things clearly, who helps rather than sells, the experience stands out. Not because it was elaborate or went far beyond what was reasonable. Because it was rare.

Good financial guidance, offered with genuine care, is one of the rarest things in financial services. When members find it, they remember it. And they come back.

The Weight of Small Conversations

One of the persistent temptations in this kind of work is to rank interactions by their apparent significance. The mortgage conversation matters. The first car loan matters. The member navigating financial difficulty, that matters. But the quick deposit, the routine question, the member who came in for something small, those feel less consequential, and it's easy to show up in them at less than full presence.

That ranking is understandable. But it's also partially wrong.

Because you can't always know, from your vantage point, which conversation is consequential to the member sitting across from you. The deposit you processed in ninety seconds might represent something significant in their life. The routine question might be the first time they've felt comfortable enough to ask it out loud. The small interaction might be the one that makes them decide whether to come back.

The practice of advice before products doesn't apply only to the big conversations. It's an orientation, a way of approaching every interaction with curiosity and presence, regardless of the size of the transaction. Not every interaction can be deep. Not every conversation will reveal something significant. But the habit of showing up fully, of treating each member as someone whose situation is worth understanding, is what makes the practice real.

And it's what members feel, even when they don't consciously register it.

The Credit Union Mission, Made Personal

Credit unions were built around a founding conviction that deserves to be taken seriously, not just cited as branding.

The people who walk through the door are members, not customers. That distinction is not semantic. It carries a specific meaning: they belong to this institution, they're co-owners of it in a meaningful sense, and they deserve to be served by someone who is genuinely looking out for their financial well-being, not just their transaction volume.

Advice before products is how that conviction gets expressed in practice. It's the individual manifestation of an institutional mission. When a banker approaches each conversation with curiosity and care, with a genuine intention to help rather than to sell, they're embodying what the credit union was founded to be.

That's not a small thing. It's the mission, in human form, playing out in individual conversations dozens of times a day across every branch. And when it's practiced consistently, when members actually feel the difference between being a member at a credit union and being a customer at a bank, the institution fulfills its original purpose.

The Practice, Ongoing

This is the final chapter of the book. But it shouldn't feel like an ending, because the work described in these pages doesn't have an ending.

Advice-based banking is not a technique you master and then set aside. It's a practice. Something you develop over time, that gets better with experience, that occasionally lapses under pressure and has to be deliberately returned to. Something that looks different at five years of experience than it did at one year, and different again at ten.

The conversations get easier. The questions become more natural. The instinct for which direction to go deepens. But the orientation, curiosity first, understanding before advice, advice before products, has to be consciously renewed, because the pressures that push against it don't go away. The pace of the branch doesn't slow down. The scoreboard doesn't disappear. The pull toward the product remains.

What changes is the capacity to hold the practice steady in the face of those pressures. To slow down when the moment calls for it, even when the lobby is full. To ask the question rather than assuming the answer. To say the honest thing when it would be easier to say nothing. To treat the member across the desk as someone whose financial situation deserves genuine attention, regardless of what the transaction is or how busy the day has been.

That's the discipline. Simple to describe. Worth a career to develop.

Three Words

Every meaningful professional practice can be compressed, eventually, into something small, a principle or a phrase or a question that, when held in mind during the work itself, orients everything else.

For the advice-based banker, that compression is:

> *Advice before products.*

Understand the person before recommending the solution. Help them think clearly before offering the tool. Earn the right to recommend by first doing the work of understanding.

When that practice is the anchor, when it's what you return to in every conversation, in every moment where the product is tempting to reach for before the understanding is there, the rest of what this book describes follows naturally.

The questions get better. The conversations deepen. The trust forms. The relationships build. The reputation develops. The career takes shape around something real.

And the members who sat across from you, the ones who came in uncertain and left with clarity, the ones who were struggling and found a path forward, the ones who almost made a bad decision and had someone honest enough to say so, those members carry something with them that no rate or feature or promotional offer could have produced.

They carry the experience of having been genuinely helped.

That is what the work is for.

AFTERWORD

The Discipline of Member Guidance

This book has been addressed, throughout, to the individual banker. To the person sitting across the desk from a member, navigating the space between a stated request and a real need, deciding in real time whether to reach for the product or ask one more question.

That's the right place to start. Because member guidance, the discipline this book is built around, begins at that level. It begins in individual conversations, in the habits of individual bankers, in the small decisions made dozens of times a day in branches across the country.

But it doesn't end there.

The Institutional Dimension

Member guidance is the first discipline of banking, not just for the banker, but for the institution itself.

Think about what that means structurally. Before a loan is underwritten, someone had to understand the member's goal. Before a credit decision is made, someone had to help the member think clearly about what they were asking for and why. Before a relationship deepens or doesn't, someone had to decide whether to treat that first conversation as a transaction or an opportunity to actually help.

Retail bankers are not the end of the process. They're the beginning of it. The quality of member guidance at the front of the institution shapes what flows downstream, the quality of applications, the alignment between what members want and what they're actually applying for, the degree to which members understand their obligations and are likely to honor them. Strong member guidance produces better loans, better relationships, and better outcomes at every level of the institution.

Weak member guidance, conversations that rush past understanding toward the product, interactions that process requests without engaging the situation behind them, creates problems that compound quietly over time. Members who didn't fully understand what they signed. Relationships that never formed. Trust that was never built and therefore can't be drawn on when it's needed. Risk that accumulates invisibly in the gap between what members thought they were getting and what they actually got.

> ***The discipline of member guidance is not a soft skill layered on top of real banking. It is real banking.***

It's how the institution stays connected to the people it was created to serve.

What Institutions Can Do

Individual bankers can practice this discipline on their own, and many do. But institutions shape the conditions under which the practice is either supported or quietly undermined.

The credit union that measures its bankers only by product counts is, whether it intends to or not, sending a signal about what the work is actually for. The branch that runs so fast no conversation has breathing room is making it harder to practice member guidance even for bankers who want to. The manager who never mentions the quality of member conversations, only the volume of transactions, is inadvertently defining what success means.

None of these are malicious. They're the natural drift of institutions optimizing for what's easy to measure. Products are easy to count. Relationships are not. Transaction speed is visible on a dashboard. The depth of a member conversation is not. And so, over time, institutions can end up rewarding the measurable at the expense of the meaningful, without ever deciding to, without anyone explicitly choosing that outcome.

The organizations that practice member guidance most consistently are the ones that have made deliberate choices about what they measure and recognize. They track member return rates and referral patterns alongside product counts. They celebrate bankers who members ask for by name. They make time in training and coaching conversations for the quality of guidance, not just the quantity of transactions. They treat the discipline of member guidance not as optional enrichment but as core to how they define their work.

That's institutional leadership. And it matters.

The Credit Union Difference

Credit unions occupy a specific and unusual position in the financial services landscape. They are member-owned cooperatives, institutions whose structure reflects a founding conviction that people deserve a financial institution that is genuinely on their side.

That conviction is not just historical. It's present. It's the reason credit unions exist as a distinct category, and it's the reason the members who walk through the door carry a different expectation than the customers of a commercial bank. They're not just using a service. They belong to something. And belonging carries an expectation, implicit, rarely stated, but real, that someone at this institution actually cares about their financial well-being.

Advice before products is how that expectation gets met. It's the practice-level expression of the cooperative mission. When a credit union banker approaches a member conversation with genuine curiosity, with the intention of understanding before recommending, with the willingness to say the honest thing even when it's uncomfortable, they're not just doing their job well. They're fulfilling the institution's founding purpose.

And when credit unions do this consistently, when the member experience actually reflects the member-first mission rather than just invoking it, something important happens. Members notice the difference. They stay. They refer others. They bring more of their financial life to the institution. The credit union grows not by competing on rates or convenience but by being genuinely useful in a way that other institutions aren't.

That's the competitive advantage the founding model was always pointing toward. Not a lower rate. A better relationship.

The Broader Stakes

It's worth stepping back even further for a moment, because the stakes here extend beyond any individual credit union or banker.

Most people navigate their financial lives without access to genuinely good guidance. They make significant decisions, about debt, about housing, about savings, about risk, based on incomplete information, on instinct, on what they read online, on conversations with friends and family who know roughly as much as they do. The financial services industry has the infrastructure to help. The knowledge is there, the access points exist, the relationship is already established. What's often missing is the willingness to use that access for genuine guidance rather than product placement.

When bankers practice member guidance consistently, when they slow down, ask the right questions, help members understand their options, and tell them the honest thing, they're filling a gap that matters. Not just to the individual member in that conversation, but to the household that member goes home to, the family that depends on the financial decisions they make, the community whose economic health is shaped in part by the quality of the financial decisions its members make.

This is not grandiose. It's the quiet, cumulative effect of thousands of conversations, done well, over time. One member who understood what they were signing. One family who avoided taking on more debt than they could handle. One person who came in overwhelmed and left with a realistic path forward. Multiplied across every branch, every banker, every year.

> ***The individual conversation is small. The aggregate is not.***

The Work Ahead

Every banker reading this book is somewhere on the journey from transaction to relationship, from product-first to guidance-first, from competent professional to trusted advisor.

The journey doesn't have an endpoint. There's no moment where the practice is complete and the discipline is fully mastered. There are only more conversations, each one an opportunity to choose curiosity over assumption, understanding over guessing, honesty over convenience.

What changes with experience is not the nature of the practice but the ease of it. The questions come more naturally. The instinct for what a member needs sharpens. The discomfort of saying the honest thing in a difficult conversation eases, because you've seen enough times that it was the right call. The confidence deepens, not the performed confidence of someone managing a transaction, but the genuine confidence of someone who knows what they're doing and why it matters.

And the relationships accumulate. Slowly, invisibly, one conversation at a time, until the work begins to feel like something more than a job. Until the branch feels like a place where real things happen for real people. Until the member who walks in looking for you specifically, who scans the room, finds you, and settles, is not a remarkable event but a regular one.

That's what the discipline produces, practiced over time. Not a credential. Not a title. Not a scoreboard number.

A practice. A reputation. A career built on something that lasts.

A Final Word

The Advice-Based Banker is the first book in The Discipline of Banking series. The conversations described in these pages, between a member and a banker, at the beginning of every financial decision, are the foundation on which everything else in a financial institution rests.

The books that follow will address the other disciplines: how credit is structured, how risk is monitored over time, how leaders are developed, how institutions are stewarded. Each discipline matters. Each shapes the health and effectiveness of the institution.

But member guidance comes first. Not because it's more important than the others in some absolute sense, but because it's where every financial relationship begins. The discipline of understanding members before recommending solutions, of helping people think clearly before offering tools, of earning trust through genuine guidance rather than efficient processing, this discipline is the root from which everything else grows.

Practice it well.

The Discipline of Banking Series

Banking is often described as a business of products, policies, and transactions. In reality, it is a business of judgment.

Every day, bankers help members make financial decisions, design loans that must work over time, monitor risk as conditions change, and lead institutions through uncertainty. When judgment is inconsistent, risk accumulates quietly. When judgment is disciplined, institutions become resilient.

The Discipline of Banking Series exists to clarify that judgment.

Each book focuses on one discipline required for strong financial institutions: guiding members toward sound decisions, structuring credit carefully, recognizing risk before it becomes visible, forming capable leaders, and stewarding institutions with responsibility.

These disciplines are simple, but they are not automatic. They must be practiced intentionally across the organization.

Good banking is not a moment of approval or a single transaction.

It is a continuous act of judgment.

The Discipline of Banking Series

For Retail Bankers	**The Advice-Based Banker** The Discipline of Member Guidance **Banking the Business** The Discipline of Knowing your Business Customer **Lead With Lending** The Discipline of Delivering for Members
For Commercial Lenders	**Loan By Design ™** The Discipline of Loan Structure **The Cash Discipline ™** The Discipline of Operating Cash
For Commercial Loan Portfolio Manager	**The Quiet Risk Manager ™** The Discipline of Credit Stewardship in Commercial Lending
For High Performing Leaders	**The Assembled Leader ™** The Discipline of Leadership Formation in Regulated Industries
For Executive Teams and Boards	**The Leadership Tax ™** The Discipline of Capacity Stewardship
For Everyone	**Money In. Money Out. Risk Stays.** How Credit Unions Work, From the Inside

This Book's Role in the Discipline of Banking

The **Discipline of Banking** describes the core disciplines that determine whether financial institutions perform well over time.

Each book in the series examines one of those disciplines in depth.

The Advice-Based Banker™ focuses on the first discipline: Member Guidance.

Before loans are structured.
Before risk is monitored.
Before strategy is debated in conference rooms.

A decision is already forming.

A member sits across from a banker and tries to make sense of a financial choice.

That conversation is where judgment first enters the system.

When bankers approach these conversations with curiosity, clarity, and disciplined advice, decisions tend to compound into trust, sound structure, and durable relationships.

When conversations are rushed, transactional, or reduced to product fulfillment, trust never fully forms, and downstream problems become more likely.

This book explains how strong bankers guide those early conversations, and why the quality of that guidance shapes everything that follows.

www.ingramcontent.com/pod-product-compliance
Lightning Source LLC
LaVergne TN
LVHW010916110826
845149LV00013B/2384

* 9 7 9 8 9 9 5 6 3 5 9 0 1 *